FALLOW ARE THE FIELDS

FALLOW ARE THE FIELDS

A Civil War Tale

Steven D. Ayres

Library of Congress Number: 2004095289
ISBN : Hardcover 1-4134-6390-8
Softcover 1-4134-6389-4

This is a work of fiction. Any name, personality, and/or character in this book is merely co-incidental with any person or persons, whatsoever, living or dead, and are only fictional in character.

This book was printed in the United States of America.

To order additional copies of this book, contact:
Xlibris Corporation
1-888-795-4274
www.Xlibris.com
Orders@Xlibris.com
23349

CONTENTS

ILLUSTRATIONS

By
The Author

This Book is dedicated to the only thing I love
Better than my Southern Heritage, My Wonderful Wife

Beth

My Own "Southern" Belle
From
Missouri
California
Maryland
Washington, D. C.
& Finally
Georgia

ACKNOWLEDGEMENTS

In bringing together this story, I have drawn upon the help and inspiration of many wonderful people, as well as the historical facts of the times.

I would like to thank all of my friends and associates who have contributed in any way to the forming of this book. Many have read the original manuscript and have offered invaluable suggestions and comments. Others have checked for historical accuracy and to see that I have stayed within the historical framework, overall.

I would like to personally thank my wife, Beth for being patient with me in this long undertaking and for her encouragement along the way. Thank you also for the help and patience of my grown children: Stephanie, Benjamin, Heather and her husband Matt McKay.

May I say thank you to all who have offered help and suggestions including but not limited to Jim Harden, Donna of the Waffle House; Shirley and Bumell Franklim, Goldia Harden, Scott Fields; Ray Henderson, Shirley Carden, Elaine and John Bailey, Robert Guy, Brenda and David Fain, Ruth Gilmer, Jerry and Susan Frith, Danny and Carol Beck, Monroe King; my mother and father in-law, Mary and Olen Hill; my parents, T. G. "Bill", and Blanche Ayres, and many others as this work progressed. Thank you also to Amiee Adams and Jeremiah Adams for your interests, kind words and efforts in bringing this story to a broader circle of people.

In closing "Thank You" to anyone and everyone who had even a small influence in the happening of this book. I pray that the South and its great heritage will always be as good to you as it has been to me and my family. God Bless You All and God Speed.

The Author

PREFACE

This is a fictional story based in historical facts woven together with pen and heart. The broader story is certainly true and profound and the more personal story was probably true even if untold before or undocumented. It altogether documents the transition in the South during the American War Between the States and chronicles the dying out of a culture—a way of life—as it relates what happened to a single family.

I know this story, this terrain and the facts because I live here today with my family, 140 years later, on the very site where these historical events occurred. I live today on the old farm just three miles west of Salt Springs, today Lithia Springs, Georgia. As a boy I drank from the same springs and swam in the same creeks and plowed the same fields. Sometimes, when I sit quietly on the bank of Sweetwater Creek beside the ruins of New Manchester Mill, I can almost hear the clatter of the machinery as clearly as the running waters of the still rushing Factory Shoals. The shape of the land and the curves of the creek are the same now as they were then. Much of this land today, in this story, is protected as Sweetwater Creek State Park and Kennesaw Mountain National Military Park. The places in between are still, as then, unprotected, unpretentious and as common as the ground upon which we walk. Today, the names are only engraved lines on tombstones and are faded black entries on old census records. Triumphs and tragedies are only epithetic reminders on yellow tattered newspapers. But, as I walk the once fallow fields of my ancestors I can still see their story unfolding before me.

Steven D. Ayres

CHAPTER 1

The Family

I grew up in the low hills of Northwest Georgia. It was a time when the world was much smaller than it is now. Days and weeks seemed to last forever and the entire universe centered around the family farm. The year I was born was 1846, in the month of July, day of the 6th. Momma always said I was almost a firecracker since I just missed Independence Day by two days.

The family farm wasn't really big by most standards. It was just your ordinary one-horse farm. My dad always preferred a horse over a mule 'cause he said you didn't have to talk to a horse the same way you did a mule. A horse was, he said, almost as smart as a human being, but, I don't know where he got his information because some human beings I know sure don't have much sense.

Well, we had all the regular things little North Georgia farms had I guess, like barns, chickens, a few cows, a couple of pigs, and, of course, the horse. We even had four hound dogs. Two were big old blue ticks, one was a big yellow hound, and the other was an old, old white bitch hound, the mother of the other three. The daddy was, as my maw told it, the traveling-salesman-kind-of-dog and we never seen him but three times ever. Then there was the pet coon that my sister took up with, or should I say, he took up with her.

The Old Farmstead
North Georgia Hills

Our house wasn't real fancy but it kept most of the wind off of you in the winter time. It was an old clap board siding house, covered with heart-of pine lumber. Matter of fact, the entire house I suppose was built from heart-of-pine; built to last a lifetime for several generations. We didn't build it, but a man named Mr. Duncan built it about ten years or so ago. After a couple of years, his wife died with the pox and since they never had any children he just up and decided to sell to my paw. Made a real good trade, my paw did, from what I been told. We got the whole 400 acre farm for the price of two horses, a two-horse wagon, and half of the crops for the first two years, good or bad. The only thing we didn't know was how many rocks this old farm could grow. It seemed that every time we plowed an inch of ground two rocks would grow out without you even have'n to plant 'em. We just couldn't eat rocks, that was the bad thing. After a while though, we learned to do a lot of things with those rocks. They made good piles, real pretty like, and when we needed some we always knew where to get them. Yea, we used them for other things too, as foundations for buildings, walls, chimneys and the like. We even built an entire spring house out of 'em and a storm and root cellar too.

And we had a well. A good well too with one of those little house roofs built over the top, so as to keep the rain water out I guess. At least you could draw water in the rain and not get wet, except for comin' and goin' to the well. On sunny hot days it was rather nice and was pretty good in the snowy weather too, what little snow we got.

Now, I really didn't say too much about the house cause it actually wasn't much to talk about. It was your basic run down old house of four rooms with a wood burning fireplace on each end, so as to keep the two ends of the house warm in the winter and the rest somewheres between chilly to barely above freezin'. I hardly ever remember ice in the house during the winter time; but it wasn't all together uncommon if nobody 'tended the fires for a few days, like if we were all out huntin' or somethin'. My maw liked to keep a small fire goin' 'most all the time, even when it was hot so she could make tea or coffee or biscuits. She cooked on the open hearth for most of my childhood until we finally built her a kitchen on the north side of the house with its own cooking fireplace. We couldn't afford a cook stove, like some people in the towns had, until I was fifteen years old.

The land around our farm was some of the most beautiful land on God's green earth. At least we thought it was. Fields and trees and streams running through big virgin hardwoods and more game than you could use almost. Deer, rabbits, squirrels, quail, and all the wild berries' and fruits you can imagine. Between all that, and the crops and domestic animals, there wasn't much we lacked for in the way of food. Of course we did buy our sugar, what little we used, and we bought our coffee and tea. Our corn was ground down at the local mill, run by the Abernathy brothers, and made into cornmeal and our wheat made into flour. Two freshened cows kept us in all the milk and butter and buttermilk we could use. Two dozen chickens usually produced about a dozen to a dozen and a half of eggs nearly every day. So we ate pretty good.

Nothing like eatin' a hot sweet potato, right out of the fire, with hot meltin' butter drippin' allover it. Makes your mouth water just thinkin' about it, don't it!?

Low mountains hung off in the distance to the north. Local folks called them the Allatoona Mountains, foot stools to the bigger Blue Ridge Mountains, all part of the southern range of the great Appallachin Mountains. And, we had a couple of smaller but very impressive hills just to the north of our farm. One of those hills was called Lost Mountain, and the other bigger hill was actually a real mountain I guess, cause they called it Kennesaw Mountain. It was named after the little railroad settlement of Kennesaw or maybe that was somebody's name, I don't know. But what I do know is about Lost Mountain. The Indians named it that because when you looked at it from a distance it really did look like a mountain, but, when you got up to it, it was gone. I mean like it was really lost, you couldn't find it. Except you really could, it just wasn't no mountain anymore. It was more like a mole hill. Now, just off to the northeast of Lost Mountain was another little mole hill called pine mountain and then off to the northeast of Kennesaw Mountain was another good size hill called Brushy Mountain.

Now all this doesn't mean much right now, but as this story continues you'll see that all these mountains and mole hills had quite a significant impact on what finally happened around the family farm.

In 1846 when I was born, the world seemed to be a mighty peaceful place to live. Provided you ignore the Mexican War and the War of 1812. Compared to what was coming these were just uncivil past times. Military exercises to prepare the powers that be for some real downright and dirty fighting. A civil war it was later to be called by some. To tell the truth, I never ever saw not one thing that was "civil" about it. As most people, referred to it as the "War Between The States," or the "late great unpleasantness" as some old women called it. But I can tell you, for one, that it was definitely the most "uncivil" war that you can imagine. A sure 'nuff war between the Confederate States of America and the United States of America. The rebels, as we were called, and the yankees or Federals, as they was called. Down to the last man I tell you, we were all Americans and why we were fighting the way we were is a little bit beyond my country-boy comprehension. Well, some said it was for slavery and some said it was because of slavery, and some said it was for state's rights and some said it was because of state's rights. I don't know. We didn't own no slaves but now my grandpappy did up in South Carolina, my mother's father. and his father did too. Up to about 300 I think. It took a lot of labor to run rice plantations and at one time, I think they owned three different ones up on the Cooper River near Monk's Corner.

My mother told me all about them losing the family fortune somehow and how her daddy had grown up there on the plantation and such. But I never knew him very good as I had only known him as a very young child.

Nevertheless the fighting got started somehow. I guess when someone shoots at you, it's only natural to return the fire and shoot back, and before you know it you got the whole darn country shooting backwards and forwards at each other. And you never knew who was who as far as being a foreigner or somethin' 'cause we was all brothers, and fathers, and sons, and such. The only difference you could tell was whether they was wearing blue or if they was wearing gray. Sometimes the shades changed, like butternut gray or light shady blue but you could pretty well tell. Especially if they was already pourin' lead your way. Didn't matter too much what you looked like as long as you were still able to look at all.

Four years on the march away from home, back in forth allover the country, away from your loved ones and the comforts of home was almost more than anyone person could ever take. Camp life was mostly borin' and the biggest danger was gettin' sick. If you was to get sick you had nearly four times the chance of dying as going into battle and getting the middle blown outa you with a miniball. No sir, you sure didn't want to get sick in camp or while on the march. Hospitals were nonexistent for all practical purposes and if you did ever see any they was so full of the wounded and dying that they wouldn't have any room for you anyway, so you either got well or you might as well go ahead and die. So many boys got sick and it was so sad to know that there was so little you could do to help. One time I remember when I got sick with fever, just a burnin' up I was and hardly a kind hand to bring me a drink of water. For three days I wished I had died and finally through some miracle I just popped up and was fine.

Yes, the war was a terrible time. It was somethin' you don't ever forget in a million years. And it affected everybody not just the soldiers. It affected, at least here at home, all the civilian population allover the South and a good bit of the North too. It wasn't a pretty time and it wasn't a wonderful experience like we all thought it was going to be. But it was exciting. Terrifying is really a more accurate description. I never been so scared in all my life as I was more than a dozen times during that war. There's just no describing what war is really like. One day you're one place and the next day you're somewhere else, always on the move when there was action, then in camp for weeks and months sometimes when nothing else was happening, a time when the generals were sorting out their battle maps and trying to match their wits with their backsides.

Now, I didn't tell you about all my family back home in the early years. When I was born I already had four older brothers. The oldest was named William Gordon, and we called him will because he was so strong-willed. He was big and strong and very spiritual-like, havin' to be the oldest and all. I guess he had to have all the wisdom for the rest of us kids and he looked out for us just like ma and pa would. He was a handsome fellow and my ma and pa both thought that the sun rose and set on his shoulders. They was real proud of William.

Then there was Levi, the next oldest, who could plow a field in one day's time. I mean a big field too. I never seen anybody who could get the work done like Levi and he loved animals too. Had a certain way with them he did. Not like most people who didn't understand what animals were about. Next there

was Samuel, who we just called Sam most of the time. Sam was a different kind of kid who never liked to work much, but he could do things that the rest of us couldn't do, like work with words and pictures. He'd draw a picture, then write a little story to go with it like in a book or something. Ma taught us to read the Good Book and that's where most of his stories and drawings would come from, although he often took somethin' from right out of his head and just come up with it. He'd get ideas from the farm too. He always did the milkin' cause he said it gave him time to think.

The brother just older than me was Benjamin, we called him Ben. He was just about a year or so older than me and we were pretty close. Much closer in some respects than the others, although we were all mighty close when it came to lookin' out for and protectin' one another. Ben, though, was special in his own special way 'cause me and him were just like two fingers pointed in the same direction. He was smart, smarter than me I'm sure, but, he never acted like it. He could take apart and put back together anything that existed. He was 'specially good with taking care of the guns. Our huntin' rifles and pistols were always in tip top shape 'cause Ben made it his job to see to that. If ever anything' broke, no matter what it was, Ben would fix it better than new.

Then there was me, my name was Steven but everybody in the family called me Stevie, at least when I was little. I guess 'cause I was the baby until my little sister came along. I was mother's pet I think. At least I like to think I was. She was always doting on me and lookin' out for me I suppose, as I was somewhat precocious and always get tin' into things. I just loved bein' curious about things and often got myself into trouble when I found out it was a lot easier to take things apart than it was to put them back together. Thank goodness for Ben who could bail me out. You see I just had a very imploring mind and liked to look at things from inside out.

The real baby of the family was my kid sister, Anna, who was the most beautiful little blonde headed girl this side of the Mississippi River, probably the other side too. There was nothing that Anna wanted that Anna didn't get. Talk about spoiled, bein' with five older brothers and all. Ma and Pa kinda spoiled on her too, being the only girl in such an otherwise rough and tumble family. I guess every family ought to have at least one girl in it to sort of help balance things out some. But, she was just like us, or at least she wanted to be. She was nothing but a tomboy all made up like a girl, and although we treated her like one of the guys we knew she was only a girl. We loved her though and there wasn't anything or anyone ever gonna cause her no harm. We made sure of that.

Life was hard back then, or so it seemed at times. But now looking back, I know it was really easy 'cause everything was all planned out for you to do nearly all the time. I mean, what with the clearin', and plowin', and milkin', feedin' and wood cut tin' and a million and one things that had to be done on the farm. Of course, with a family the size of mine there were not only a lot of mouths to feed, but there was a lot of hands to help do the work. So, it wasn't so bad. We were like our own little army of ants doing everything that had to be done and we loved every minute of it. My Pa and Ma would see to that! Anything to keep us busy 'cause idle hands made for idle minds or so they said. I wouldn't know 'cause I never got that idle.

If we weren't working on some project or doing regular chores, we was a fishing or hunting, spending time in the deep woods, or down by the pond or on the creek bank. Summertime we were all swimming whenever we got the chance to cool off in the hot afternoons, usually on Saturday or Sunday or both. Of course, Sunday was the meeting day at church every other Sunday. We couldn't get a full-time preacher so we had a part-time preacher, but ma always said we was still suppose to have full-time religion all the time. On Sundays when the preacher didn't come, ma would gather us all around on Sunday morning just like church anyway, and she would read to us from the Good Book and talk to us about being good and loving one another and forgiving one another and things like that. If there was ever one thing my mother taught us it was "Love". Not just love, love, but real deep-seeded love in your heart, the kind that she said God always has for you. You know, the kind of love that loves you even when you don't deserve it for nothing. I remember a particular lesson one Sunday that she shared with us that I never will forget. She said if you take God's loving Grace and you spell the word GRACE out, that each letter stands for a word, an acronym I think she called it. And that was, that God Receives All his Children without Exception, and she did too. This just seemed powerful to me and I never forgot it. That stood by for me too when it came my turn to go off to war. Regardless of what we do and who we are, that God still loves us just like our parents, even when we don't deserve it. Not a bad thought to live by I figured. If I too could live and love with God's Grace in my life, I'd do allright and I have.

I want to say a few things about my pa too. He, first of all, was a good man who looked after all of us mighty good. We never went hungry and we never lacked really for anything we really needed. Sure we thought we needed some things but we didn't really, we just wanted them. Like the time I wanted a new rifle when I was about twelve. He said I was still a mite young and needed to be a little older. But heck, I had been shootin' and a huntin' since I was old enough to pull a trigger out there on the farm. Well I pleaded and begged for I don't know how long until finally one day he called me over by the fireside one morning. I'll never forget, and he said "Stevie' I know you're young and still kinda little, but you've been a good boy and you've been responsible about things, and I've got a surprise for you. I knew you've always wanted to have your own gun, so son I'm gonna give you Grandpa's old shotgun here. He took it down from over the mantle over the old rock fireplace and he placed it in my hands. And he said, son, this old shotgun you know was your grandpa's old shotgun, and it means a lot to me. When I was just a young boy my daddy gave it to me to look after and take care of and now son I'm passing it on to you. My face lit up like the Fourth of July and my heart swelled with pride as I took it into my own hands knowing that now it was mine. My own gun to take care of and to shoot and hunt with and to protect. It was the nearest thing I guess I've ever experienced to really feel like I was going into manhood. It was an awesome time and an awesome experience to know that my pa trusted me with one of the things that meant the most to him and I would cherish it forever.

The Family Meal

CHAPTER 2

The Oncoming War

The days were long in the hot summer months of June, July and August. Everybody, everywhere was talking about secession from the union. Some couldn't wait to see us all get out of the union and have our own state or country. Georgia was no exception to the cry for sovereignty. I never heard so many arguments and so much confusion over who was right and who was wrong. Slavery was talked about a lot especially up in the north, mostly by people who didn't even have any slaves. Abolitionists they was called by most folks. I didn't really understand what all the fuss was about 'cause we sure didn't have no slaves on our farm. But nearly all the big plantations had slaves. Cotton was "King" and the slaves were the labor for picking that cotton. Some masters had as many as a hundred or more. Sometimes a lot more. Even though we didn't own any, I knew that my great grandpa and my grandpa had owned as many as three hundred and somethin' up in Charleston, South Carolina. Yeah, I guess we had been a part of all the ruckus too. On that plantation up at Monk's Corner, Lewisfield Plantation, named after the original owner on the Cooper River, my grandpa on my mother's side had had a slew of slaves to help run the rice plantation. As a matter of fact, they had owned three rice plantations all together along the Cooper River just up from Charleston. Because my great grandpa had the good fortune to marry a girl, being the daughter of another plantation owner who owned two plantations. So I guess in our family, rice was, if not king, at least was a queen. Matter of fact, there was hardly a day went by that we didn't have rice for at least one meal. But I never saw any of these slaves 'cause we never went up to Charleston when I was growing up, something had happened a few years earlier that caused the family to lose all the plantations and everything that went with them. My great grandma had died leaving all three plantations with my grandpa who later remarried, unfortunately so my new great grandma, no blood relation, became a step-mother to my grandpa and his brother. Soon afterwards, their father died, leaving them to be raised under the eye of the step-mother who really didn't give a pea turkey what happened to them. She had a child by a former marriage who she doted on and gave all her attention to. Now my great grandpa, in his will, had left Lewisfield Plantation to my grandpa and his brother, who were both minors at the time. A shrewd, smart, and I might say crooked Charleston lawyer was the executor of his estate. He did see that the boys were cared for and got everything they needed, but in the meantime all the wealth of the estate was used up and the plantation fell into disuse and was actually abandoned for some time. As the taxes piled up it just didn't seem practical I guess to pay on something that wasn't producing at the time and the old lawyer just milked it for all it was worth then let it go. First thing you know the plantation was sold to satisfy taxes and some old codger from Maryland bought it on the courthouse steps for next to nothin'. And that my friend was the end to the great "Rice" dynasty of my early family. So you see, slavery sure was not an issue to me and my family now.

Now, States rights were another thing. Nearly everybody I knew said that we had a right to do what we garl-danged pleased and that no stuffed shirt in a monkey suit from Washington was going to tell us what we could do and couldn't do. No sirree. Iffin' we wanted to have slaves, that was our own garl—darn business, and we could own them just like we owned that mule over there. After all we bought them, paid for 'em with our own hard earned money, fed 'em, cared for 'em, gave 'em a place to sleep and somethin' to do all day so as to ease their savage minds.

Now, I want you to know personally I don't take to that kind of thinkin', but a lot of people did back then. If you ask me, a black man had just as much right to be free as I did. To have a family and maybe a little farm so he could feed his family, and not have his wife and children sold away from him whenever some master wanted to. Yes, it seems to me that freedom is somethin' that belongs to every human being. But you know, blacks in those days weren't exactly considered "human beings" unfortunately. They was just considered chattel or personal property. Why the word "chattel" might just well have meant "cattle" for all the proprietary of the word. At any rate, these things were a fact, back then, not just some made up thoughts of the imagination. I heard tell of an uncle even over in Alabama who was a slave trader who made a lot of money in the slave market before the war. Didn't matter to us none though 'cause we never seen any of the money and besides we did think it was wrong

Well, talk of secession and possible war went on for some time. That summer, especially, was hotter in more ways than one. It was actually kinda exciting like, thinking that hey, maybe we might have an actual war or something. It was hard to imagine that it could happen, but times were uncertain and nobody really knew what would be the final outcome of it all. If the northerners would just let us alone, everything would be fine and dandy, but that probably was not going to happen.

Georgia seemed to be caught up in the middle of it all, I think. What with Virginia and South Carolina a hoopin' and a hollerin' all about state's rights all the time. And then there was Alabama on the other side and Mississippi and Texas who were all get tin' pretty vocal about it all. Then there was the sovereign state of Tennessee who said they would do what ever they wanted to, no matter who said what. Only thing was, a lot of people in Tennessee didn't seem to know what they wanted. They didn't have all the rich cotton land that the lower states had and things just looked a little different to them up in all those hills they had allover the place. But, one thing for sure was, they did identify with the South and probably whatever all the other southern states did they probably would too. It was kinda the same with Kentucky.

Missouri never could make up its mind, and all they could

ever do was fuss and fight eventually allover the state. You talk about a state of confusion, Missouri was it.

Then there was Florida, the state of flowers ma called it. I don't know 'cause I never had been there, but they said it was real pretty-at the ocean 'specially and there was all the sand in the world in Florida. So much sand you didn't even have to look for it. It was allover the place like snow in the winter in North Georgia. Well, Florida, we all thought was sort of a sissy state being where it was and all, and being almost surrounded by water. We knew that from our geography in school learning. The only real importance it would have in the event of any war would be 'cause of all that water around it. Shipping would be bound to be effected and this could be important to the South. Also, it was the backdoor to the South and it would be a fine way to stab the south in the back if ever the north could be pass our front door. Fat chance they'd ever have of doin' that. Anyway, Florida was obliged to do whatever the other southern states did because it really had no choice anyway.

North Carolina was bound to the south like a button on a boot. There wasn't anywhere the rest of the south was goin' without North Carolina being right there too. Right beside little sister, South Carolina. The coastal areas of the Carolinas and the naval stores of pine, pitch, and tar up in the inlands were going to be mighty important to the south in any future contest between sides.

The talk around town, out little town of Salt Springs, Georgia, was pretty brash about the possibility of secession and even war if that was what it was all to come to. Most folks didn't want war but if that was what it took, then most folks were anxious to get on with it. After all, everybody knew it would be no contest between us and them. Whoever them was. Yankees mostly. You know, it was like two kids on the street arguing about marbles and the first thing you know, ever' body was a takin' sides getting ready for the biggest brawl you ever did see.

We didn't get to town too much, but when we did, everybody would stand around the post office at the Bowden house where Judge Bowden and his family lived and talk about how we were gonna show them Yankees what we was made of. If we did go to war it wouldn't last long before we wiped the daylights out of them bastards and gave them really what for. And it seemed that everybody wanted in on the action, like it was all going to be over before they got their own personal chance to kill them a few Yankees so they could brag about it. I never seen anything like it, the way people talked. Didn't make much sense to me, but what did I know. I was just a simple country boy on the edge of a great event. Somewhere, and sometime we would all get our own personal chance to contribute to this great adventure before it was allover. We never knew just how much we'd get to see and do over the next four years or so. There was even talk about get tin' up a regiment of soldiers right here in Salt Springs. They was going to be called, "The Salt Springs Regulars." Groups were already forming up allover the area, like down at Campbellton, the County Seat of our Campbell County and companies beginning to form at Dark Corners, Winston, Sandtown and Sweetwater Town and maybe down at New Manchester Mill where a small town had grown up around New Manchester Manufacturing Co.. Factory Shoals, it was called, where they had built a five story yarn mill, the biggest in the whole state at the time. Only time would tell when all these boys would gather round from allover the country and this great conflict would begin in earnest.

CHAPTER 3

Signing Up

Nowhere were things more exciting than around the family farm three miles west of Salt Springs. With a family the size of mine there was bound to be a lot of talk and figuring on who was going to do what. All my brothers wanted to jump right in the fray before they missed out on this once in a life time adventure. They all just figured we'd all get in there together, whip the Yankees in a few weeks and we'd be back on the farm before spring planting.

William being the oldest, decided that he would lead the way and without telling ma or pa, or anyone else, he went down to Salt Springs and signed up with the Salt Springs Regulars. By now a small camp was beginning to form down on the banks of Sweetwater Creek just south of town. My pa was real proud that William was the first to take a positive step toward doing something. My ma was, of course, pretty shakin' up about it 'cause she knew our family had a lot to lose if this thing didn't turn out like we thought. And it was just so difficult for a mother to think of her boys going off to fight in some such ruckus war as this. Actually, Will, wouldn't have to report for another week, that was, so as to give you time to get your loose ends together, get whatever gear up you might have, including your guns and knives and such, and time to say your rightful good-byes to your family and friends. I think it also gave you the opportunity to brag a little too about how you was going off to war and all.

Part of the reason that will signed up was because on Sunday meeting day at the church, the preacher preached so hard about our homes and families, and how it was our "Divine Right" and responsibility to fight for and protect what was ours and our way of life. The preacher said that Hell itself could be right here on this earth iffin' we didn't stand up and do what was right. Little did he know then, that we'd have Hell to pay for what was to come anyway. Well, that preacher was probably responsible for some dozen or more good boys going down to the camp on Monday morning to get signed up in the Confederate Army.

Some people up north were calling us rebels and said this was nothing more than an out and out rebellion by the southern states that by now had formed a Confederation, they called it, an agreement to stand together, come what may, fighting or not. And the new Confederation was to be called the Confederate States of America, just like a brand new country. After all, the united States of America was the same thing when we broke off from England and all those English dandies. Great Britain, the greatest power on the face of the earth, at that time, couldn't stop us then, even with all their power and armies and navies, so who was to say that now we just couldn't do the same. Everybody thought it was a mighty fine idea to have our own country. After all, we really were different from the northerners. There was lots of differences when you come right down to it. Like how we were brought up and the way we lived and how we looked at life in general. Most of us boys grew up on farms and we ran in the woods a huntin' and playin' all the time. The woods and fields were our first and second homes. We knew how to shoot and hunt and fish and do all the things you had to know to survive in the wild.

Why, most of them northern boys all grew up in cities and towns. Well, maybe not every single one of them, but most of them did. I mean, listen, some of 'em boys were from New York City. Now, what do you think they knew about being in the woods and living off the land and such. Nothing! Nothing, I tell you!. They was a bunch of sissies, if ever I did see one. Why everybody said right off, it would take ten of them to make one of us when it came to matching wits and guts. Later, we'd find out they had plenty of wits and guts, although we never let on that we knew that. There would be some hard fightin' men to come up and out of that army, and that was for sure.

There was some things that the north really did have in favor of them though. And that was almost everything, except will power. They had more men, they had more guns, more industry, more cannons, more food, more ships, more everything! The resources they had far out numbered all that we had except, maybe our slave labor, but what good was that going to do us now? Blackies wouldn't be fightin' for the south. No way:' I don't know, I guess we'd just have to take care of 'em some how. They would come in handy in digging trenches and other defense fortifications, some thought. But who was going to need all that.

Over the next week, much talk went on in the family about who was going to do what. Samuel and Levi, especially, were set on signing up too. So, finally, my pa and ma called for a family meeting on Friday night, so we all could discuss our plans. It was agreed that some of us needed to stay and keep the farm and all going and to take care of ma and Anna. It was further agreed that Samuel and Levi would go and sign up together since they were the next two oldest boys, and the rest of us, me and Ben and Pa, and of course Anna, would stay with ma on the farm, at least for now. So this was the plan. In a few weeks, or certainly within a few months, Will and Samuel and Levi would all be back on the farm again. Or so we thought.

So, on Saturday morning pa and me and Ben went with Sam and Levi over to the sign up camp on Sweetwater Creek. We wanted to see them off and get in on part of the excitement and all. Boy were we all excited about all of this! The camp was growing with more and more boys coming in from allover the area. Captain Maxwell signed them up and turned them over to a Sergeant Gunn, who we all knew to be a pretty rough and tumble sort of man, who used to run the mill down at Mitchell Creek. Sergeant Jerome Gunn, he was a fine and stout man of good character. As a matter of fact, he was the Sergeant for Company C of the Salt Springs Regulars, the same outfit that William was in. We didn't know right then, but this regiment was to become a part of the lst Georgia Volunteers. Their Lieutenant was a fine gentleman name of Buford H. Fordham. It was to be a fine regiment and we were all so proud of them.

CHAPTER 4

The Long Wait

It wasn't but a short time that we got word that the camp had moved out, somewheres toward Atlanta. Not all that far, but sure far enough when you're talking about your family being gone.

Atlanta was a real city now by most standards. About ten thousand people lived there, and to me that seemed like all the people in the world. I guess about half of them would be off to fight in the war. Maybe not that many but then I wasn't quite sure about numbers. Maybe a fourth of them would go. Anyway, Atlanta, had really grown into quite a city because of the railroads.

Originally, the railroad out of Augusta had terminated or just plain stopped there because of the Chattahoochee River, so they just called the point, Terminus. A small settlement soon grew up with a trading post called Whitehall's and a little tavern run by Mr. Mitchell. First thing you know, everything around there was Whitehall Street, and Mitchell Street and Peachtree Street, after Mr. Mitchell's young peach orchard which seemed to go out in all directions. The road to Decatur came in about the same point where all the other roads did and soon it just became the dead center of town. Some people even called it Five Points. It's a wonder the town didn't take up that name, but it didn't. It's also surprising it wasn't called Peachtree City, but it wasn't. A few years later, the mayor had a little darling baby girl and he and the town council decided to rename the town Martharsville after his daughter. Well, the little girl either turned out not to be so wonderful or something else happened, 'cause a few years later the name was changed to

Atlanta, and that stuck. Now, where the name, Atlanta, came from I'm not exactly sure. It's a real mystery, but I always thought it had something to do with Atlantis, the lost city. But who knows. Atlanta certainly was lost, if ever there was an unlikely place to have a city this was it. No port of the sea, no port on the river. The Chattahoochee River was not navigable this far up by any big boats. The only thing that Atlanta originally had going for it was the railroad ended there and it was like the far western frontier. Of course, this was all just before I was born so what do I know. When the railroads kept building connecting up with Chattanooga, on the Tennessee River and southwesterly down to West Point on the Chattahoochee River, then Atlanta took on a whole new significance as a sort of railroad hub. Maybe some of the founding fathers, or at least the railroad people were pretty far-sighted way back then 'cause they sure did hit on a good idea that seemed awful stupid at first. Typical of government, my pa would say, except most of the time the idea stayed stupid.

Out of Atlanta to the west ran a road that most people just called the Alabama road, 'cause that was, Where it went to Alabama. Makes sense to me. It went through a settlement called Lick Skillet, where a road split off to the south to go to Sandtown and a little further to the town of Campbellton, our county seat when Campbell County was formed.

After going through Lick Skillet, the road came on through to the Chattahoochee River, where there was a ferry, called Gordon's Ferry. Then, on westward to the next little settlement, which would come to be known as Mableton, after the Mable family farm and then on out to Sweetwater Town on the banks of the Sweetwater Creek, and then just a ways across and down the creek, to what I call, my little town of Salt Springs. The next big stop off on the way to Alabama was a place called Dark Corners and Villa Rica, and then Tallapoosa, and then you was in Alabama about half way to a little place called Birmingham. We never went past Tallapoosa, so I can't tell you about what it was like beyond there.

Just north of Salt Springs, was the town of Powder Springs and Marietta where Kennesaw Mountain was near, and just south of

Marietta back toward Atlanta was the little settlement of Smyrna. South of Salt Springs was a new little settlement called New Manchester, which had grown quite a bit since they built a big five story textile mill there on the shoals of Sweetwater Creek. Later, this would have an important bearing on the war 'cause they were soon making Confederate Uniforms there.

Many of these places I've mentioned would take on whole new meaning in the upcoming war here at home. Little did we know that we didn't have to go off to fight that we could've stayed right here and done a plenty of fighting. And some of us would.

Weeks passed and we heard no word from the brothers until finally, one day we got a letter from William. He was over in the Atlanta area somewhere near Decatur and he said that he, Samuel, and Levi were all doing fine. They were getting ready to move out soon and would be headed north some wheres.

He didn't know where, but they thought it would be up north somewhere, maybe Virginia, to meet up with some more troops and go for a march on Washington. They were all pretty excited about the prospects of that. There's nothing more boring for a soldier, they said than to be all ready to go and fight and to not be able to. Frustration was a daily enemy too and you had to fight it off every day. It wouldn't be too long now before they got a chance to show their stuff.

Around home things were still somewhat normal. We sure did miss having Will, Samuel and Levi at home on the farm however, and it took a lot more effort now to get all the things done that had to be done. After all, we were all so use to being together all the time that being apart was very difficult at first. We waited every day for some new word from the front and to hear what was happening. We would get some news each week from the Campbell County Bugle which was circulated throughout the area. They got news from Atlanta and other places and were able to put together a smattering of news regarding troop movements and what everybody speculated was going to happen. I guess a lot of it was kept secret. How secret could you keep something like an army on the move though. I mean, there must be thousands of soldiers by now on both sides, all just a itchin' for a fight.

The best we could tell was that the Confederate Army was about to make a move on Washington, D. a. and that very soon there was bound to be an engagement with the enemy. We waited and waited as patient as we could, but we heard nothing from the boys gone off to war.

Finally, a letter came in at Salt Springs from William. He being the oldest son had taken on the responsibility for him and Samuel and Levi that he would do the writing for all of them and tell us back home just what was happening to them all and how they were doing.

The letter read:

June 30, 1861

Dear Ma and Pa,

Hope everyone at home is doing fine as we are all doing real good here in the army. We have traveled a great distance already and are getting very near to Washington itself. Probably in another week or so we expect to be there. Don It know exactly what will happen then, but we expect to meet up with the yankees sooner or later. Every soldier is pretty anxio us to get on with it all. This camp life is for the birds Gets awful boring sometimes.

Samuel and Levi are doing fine too and wanted me to ask you, ma, if you might be able to send us some of them sugar cookies you always make up. They sure would be good and would help remind us of home.

Levi stepped on a snake the other day down by the creek when he was filling up some canteens. It turned around and bit him on the leg. Some of the boys said it was a moccasin, but I don't think it was. We couldn't find no fang marks on him, just a sort of bruise. Anyway, we're watching it real close and he hadn't come down with any fever or anything, so I guess he's going to be ok.

Samuel said to tell you that he's getting a lot of ideas for some stories and picture drawings, but time to draw has been limited 'cause they keep us a working and drilling nearly all the day. He did want me to tell you how good he can shoot. As a matter of fact, there was some talk about him maybe getting into some Sharpshooter outfit, he is so good. Must be those baby blue eyes he has.

Well, they're about to call for lights out and we got to rise up with the sun every morning, so I reckon I'll close for now.

Be sure to tell Ben and Stevie, and Anna hello and that we miss them all and we love you all very much.

Your Loving and Devoted Son, William

CHAPTER 5

A Day of Reckoning

Every few days now, we would pick up some gossip of news about the armies. It seemed like it would be just a matter of days before there was a real battle.

We didn't really count Fort Sumter, back in April, 'cause it was a limited engagement, although, it was against a United States Garrison in Charleston Harbor. It was actually the first real fighting that went on, but it wasn't between two armies really. At least not like now was about to happen. Fort Sumter finally just surrendered, and that was the end of that. It was good for Charleston, though, 'cause of the harbor and the ships and all. But, it has been a long time on this continent since two major armies clashed, not counting the Mexican War of course, or the War of 1812.

This was going to be a different sort of war, one fought between Americans on American soil. It was bound to be considerably different. We were confident it would end in our favor and not last very long. After all, it was more like a big family brawl. We had even heard about some families splitting up over the idea of secession and slavery and the whole business. Some southerners, I heard, even went up north to join the northern army, but I don't think we actually knew of any personally.

Well, there was one real strong abolitionist from Macon who we had heard went north to Chicago to help raise up a regiment. Don't know his name right off but everyone considered him a traitor to the south and if he ever gets caught, I'm sure that he will be hanged.

Late in July, the word finally came that the southern boys had met the Yankees at a little place just south of Washington called Manassas Junction. A pleasant little creek ran through the countryside called Bull Run.

According to the reports, it seemed that all of Washington had come out to witness the great spectacle. Even dandies with their ladies came out on the hillsides in carriages and such and would you believe with picnic baskets. Some picnic this was to be. According to all the reports, the two armies went at it and fighting broke out allover the place. After a few hours, the yankees decided that they had had enough and started skedaddling back to Washington in total disarray, sometimes, even getting ahead of the spectators and carriages. It must have been one of the most unsightly scenes ever imagined.

We all knew that when it came time for a showdown that the yankees would turn tail and run. They just didn't have it in 'em to really fight. After all, what were they fighting for anyway? They didn't have no darkies to save. The only thing they had to save was their hides.

If the rest of the war went like this, it would be a short war indeed. Washington, itself, lay right before the Confederate army. Now, there was nothing to stop the advancement of this great assemblage of fighting men from allover the south. Three months tops, and this war would be over.

We thought we were unorganized, but no way compared to the Yankee or Federal Army. When they started to run; they were all over the place. There wasn't anything organized about their retreat at all. Officers were just as bad as the enlisted men. All they could do was run for their lives.

There was one thing that came out of all this confusion that seemed to help some of our boys, and that was about the flag. You see the Official Confederate Flag, the stars and bars, looked so much like the United States Flag, the stars and stripes, that half the time, some of the boys didn't know which was which. So General Beauregard decided to use a battle banner which would be easily recognizable by our boys. It was an X cross of blue with thirteen white stars on it for the southern states, bordered by white, all on a beautiful field of red. And it was almost square. "It was a wonderful looking flag," all the men said, and there was no confusion about who's flag it was. The men really seemed to like it and it has since become known as Beauregard's Battle Banner. I expect more units will begin to use it also.

The next day or so after the Battle of Bull Run, as most people began to call it, time was spent mostly removing the wounded and the dead. "It was an awful sight," it was said by those who were eye witnesses to the event. But the morale was so high by now in the southern army, that it seemed it would be an invincible force.

By the time the armies got themselves ready to fight again, it was already too late to make a direct move on Washington. In just a matter of days, the defenses around Washington had been strengthened so that it would have taken Napoleon's army itself to have broken the lines. No, for now, the Confederates would back off and regroup themselves. There would be another time for aggression. For right now, the south wanted to enjoy and bask in its great victory. Maybe after this, the north would give up and just say, "okay, we'll let you alone, go home." But this didn't happen either.

CHAPTER 6

Back Home

Meanwhile, back home, things rocked along, as they say. There got to be a considerable amount of unrest though among most people, because they didn't understand why everything was a taking so long. If you were going to fight, then do it and do it now. This dragging things out was not the southern way. But most folks just didn't understand what it takes to run a great army. I mean, you don't just up and go at the drop of a hat. And when you do go, you gotta' know where to go and when. It takes a lot of everything to sustain an army of forty to fifty thousand men.

Well, in my family, things were going pretty good, so far. Pa was working on a new field down by the lower spring. Ben and me were trying to help him as much as we could. It had been a hot summer working out there in the blazing hot sun, but at least the water spring was close by and the old gourd dipper we kept hanging on the tree above it made many a dip in the cool, clear spring water. When we'd take a break, we'd be a standing around the spring and me, and Ben, and pa would all get to talking about the war and all. We were missing out on this once in a lifetime greatest of adventures. But pa said that war wasn't all that glorious at all. That it was really a sad and awful thing to have to take a man's life so you could save your own and live by your own ideas instead of his. It was no smal consideration to do that he said. But there does come a time in a man's life when he has to stand up for what he thinks is right and if war is what it means, then that is what it takes.

He said he sure was proud of Will and Samuel and Levi and what they were doing, but he sure did miss them around the farm. "I guess we all feel that way," said Ben. "But you know pa, we want to do something too. Me and Stevie been talking about all this and you know the war is going to be over so soon and we won't even be able to say we had a part in it all. And pa, we're ready. We're ready to go and fight too, pa."

Pa just took another slow sip of the cool spring water as he thought real hard. You could always tell when pa was a thinking real hard, 'cause he didn't say a thing, he just looked like he was so calm or something. Pa kinda reminded me of our horse when he was getting shod. He just stood there at attention like, with all his power and all his purpose, and he didn't even flinch a muscle hardly, while the blacksmith went to work on all four hoofs. Pa was powerful and calm at the same time just like that. And you never knew just exactly what he was a thinking.

Pa wanted to join the army too. We knew he did 'cause you could see it in his eyes. But we couldn't tell just exactly what he was planning to do about it all. We thought that maybe he would go off and join the army and have Ben and me stay home to look after ma, and Anna, and the farm. We were old enough to take care of things. Ben was sixteen already, just barely, and I was almost fifteen, shy by just a few days.

There are just some things a man has to do at the right time and in the right place. There was more than opportunity here, there was most certainly responsibility to fight for ones homeland. It would be a difficult decision for pal for he was torn between two worlds, that is for sure. Ma would accept his decision because she understood too, deep down in her heart. Pa was a man's man and he was too proud not to do his part, whatever that was to be.

One morning late, sometime after all the chores had been done, pa came 'round the old barn with Chester, our horse, all saddled up and packed with what looked like camping gear. He called ma out and asked for Anna, and Ben, and me to all gather round. He said it was time now. His time, and he was going to find General Joseph Wheeler's Cavalry and sign up for one year. Maybe it wouldn't be all that long even.

Pa took each one of us individually and as he knelt down he hugged and kissed Anna first, then stood and hugged me and then Ben. Then he walked over to ma and embraced her like he might never see her again, he kissed her ever so gently, and then he turned around and got up on Chester. Chester was a big bay about sixteen hands high, which was a pretty big horse. He looked mighty good that morning with pa sitting up there so proud. With a quick throw of the reins, he and Chester turned and began to canter down the path to the gate. When they got to the gate pa and Chester turned, looked back for one last time, waved, turned again and cantered on down the road 'til they were out of sight.

We would really miss pa around the farm and sitting around the family fireplace, but this is how it must be and everyone knew it and understood it, except for Anna who cried a lot at first. She was only twelve years old at the time, and she didn't quite make sense of it all. She didn't know that pa had no choice but to take off for the war too.

Things around home got mighty quiet for a while with pa being gone, and Will, and Sam and Levi. We kept waiting for some word, a letter or something, but for a good while we never heard from any of them.

Then one day, on a Saturday, we had to go up to Salt Springs. Ma wanted to get some yarn so she could make some sweaters for pa and the boys, so when we found out where they were she could send them to 'em. While we were there, we checked down at the post office and Judge Bowden said there were two letters for ma that had just come in the other day and he knew we'd be anxious to get them. As a matter of fact, he was about to have them run out to the farm if we didn't show up real soon.

Ma couldn't wait 'till we got home, so out on the front porch of the post office she sat down on the steps with all us gathered 'round her to see what was the news. She opened pa's letter first.

Dearest Ginny, April 10, 1862

I wanted to write to you and let you know that I finally located General Wheeler's Calvary and got joined up over in Alabama. We were only in camp there for a few days when we got the orders to move out. And it seems we have been doing nothing but riding ever since then. My immediate commander, Major Harding is a good man who has since been wounded.

Just a few days ago we were in a major engagement at a place called Shiloh's Church. Some of the boys were calling it Pittsburg Landing being there on the Tennessee River. There was some fierce fighting went on especially in a place some of the boys called the Hornet's Nest. I think the whole place turned to a hornet's nest before it was over. I don't know for sure if I killed anyone but I'm pretty sure I must have. There was so much shooting going on allover the place it was really scary. Our main mission was to protect the railroad supply lines around Corinth, Mississippi and to keep them free from the Federals. We were constantly in and out of skirmish fights all up and down the lines. But I think we held them off like we were suppose to. It seemed like we whipped them good on the first day, but by the second day the Federals seemed to get the upper hand and we withdrew from the area. A lot of good boys on both sides went down in that awful fighting. This fellow right next to me took a miniball right in the head. I sure feel sorry for his family and all.

Tell the boys and Anna that Chester is still doing fine and hasn't taken any bullets or anything. He's ok and still riding strong.

I've got to go now, as we are fixin' to move out soon. Tell all the children I love them and miss them very much. I think you can write to me, care of Nashville, Tennessee, as I think we are headed that way. Love to all.

Your Loving and Devoted Husband,
R. B. Jett

Ma looked up and off out into space for a moment like she was lost to this world. Then all of a sudden, she quickly began to open the other letter she was holding in her trembling hands. And she began to read out loud.

Dear Ma and Pa and Family, March 15, 1862

Hope everything at home is ok and that all are doing fine. We are all ok and doin' pretty good today. We are still in Virginia under the command of General Joseph Johnston and we have made camp near the Rappahannock River. It appears, that we may encounter the enemy again soon but we don't know when or where exactly. Maybe down near Mannassas Junction again but we don't know.

Samuel and Levi send their love and ask that you all remember us in this terrible war. Fortunately, we are still in the same unit being the lst Georgia Volunteers Regiment. We're a strong regiment and we have done good on the battlefield with only minor losses. We have been very lucky so far. Please pray for us, that we will be safe and be able to come home soon.

We are all looking forward to Spring and some warmer weather, as it has been a very cold winter in the camps and on the move all the time. I'll write again as soon as I can. Love to all.

Your Loving and Devoted Sons,
William, Samuel and Levi

Ma looked up again with that starry look in her eyes. She had drifted off to that far off place again and had to bring herself back to reality.

"Well," she said," we'd best be off, we've got a lot to do. Let's get going." Ma was always like that, she wanted to be busy when things began to get on her mind. It was the only way she could handle it. She loved all us kids and pa and she longed to have us all back together again. A mother's love has got to be the strong est love on this earth, I think.

Ma said that good news called for a celebration so we could all have some peppermint from the Cowan's General Store. We did and boy did it taste good. We loved candy and didn't get it except on special occasions and ma thought that this was one of those times. As we all made our way back to the farm, we thought about the letters and talked about how it must be for pa and the boys way off somewhere, where everything was new and exciting and how awful afraid they must be sometimes about the fighting, but also how very brave they all were. We wished we were there to sort of, just to see them all and be with them. Perhaps they would be able to come home later in the summer, and we hoped and prayed that they would. That night at the supper table we all said a special prayer of thanks to the good Lord for watching out for them and taking care of our family.

CHAPTER 7

Spring Eternal

Soon the daffodils were blooming all around allover the farm and there was the sweet smell of jasmine and dogwood. Even the forever reaching and clutching honeysuckle was blossoming with its rich aroma cascading through the clear, clean spring air. The world was at peace once more for as far as we could see and smell.

Ma loved the springtime and she said it was the time for renewal of all things. She would begin to plant seeds of flowers everywhere she could because she loved the flowers so. She said they were like little children 'cept you got to see them grow up all at one time in a matter of days. Anna helped ma with the flower planting mostly. She said it was fun playing in the dirt, digging and piling, fertilizing and burying little secrets of seeds allover the place. Nobody knew where they were except her and ma and the good Lord who would look after them and bring them the angel water to quench their thirst.

Anna was a good child, a good little sister. "Somewhat precocious ma said" always getting into things, but that's the way girls are. You would have thought that Anna would still have been a tomboy, growing up around all us boys, but she wasn't much now. She was quite a little lady. Took more after ma than any of us would have ever imagined. She almost always wore a plain and simple little dress that sometimes was made from sack cloth, like the flour sacks because they were the best, and ma could sew anything she put her mind to. Made all of Anna's dresses and most of our clothes too. By age thirteen now, just on April 28, Anna was turning into more than just a young girl. Something mysteriously strange was going on allover her body and her long golden hair was looking unusually radiant in the morning sun as it glistened over her shoulder. When she went to the well to draw water she no longer walked the same way, nor did she look just the same. Like the springtime, it seemed that she too was a pretty young flower, soaking up the spring sunshine and sipping on the angel water. Her beautiful green eyes reflected the lush green countryside of north Georgia.

Anna had a beau from over at a little pea patch farm near Powder Springs. She had met him at church sometime back. His name was Luther. Luther Gates. Luther was tall and lanky and a real good size for his age which wasn't much more than Anna's. He had dark, curly, almost black hair, clean shaven, 'cause I don't think he could have grown a beard yet iffin' he wanted to. Not enough whiskers yet, or the cat kept licking them off. Luther was a handsome enough young man, pretty spit and polished when he called on Anna. Even shined his shoes once. They'd mostly just sit around on the porch swing at night and talk about nothin,'. But one thing he could do though and that was he could playa banjo and he would often bring it over in the evenings. Ma, and Ben, and me loved to hear the banjo playing 'cause it was real different from the guitar that I played and the harmonica that Ben played. When we'd get all together we could really make the dogs howl.

We'd always start off by playing Camptown Races and we nearly always finished up with a rip-roaring rendition of Dixie. Then we'd play Dixie real slow and reverent like at the very end like it was some kind of musical prayer for the boys off in the war. It'd give you goose bumps every time, especially when Ben would come in with his moaning and whining harmonica. Then weld just sit around real quiet like until somebody jumped up and said something.

It was too early for watermelon yet, but ma liked to make what we all called "Dancing custard", a kind of milky, starchy, sweet stuff, she'd cook down from white rice with fresh eggs and finally bake in the oven skillet. After that, it would have to cool down for a long time down in the spring cellar house. When it was real cool, it would be cut up like pie and served with coffee or lemonade depending on whether it was day-time or night-time. We called it "Dancing custard" cause it was so good it always made you want to dance. Ma was a great cook and could do almost something with anything. She could make a 'possum dinner look like it was fit for a Tahitian King, just like in our school book. One time she fixed this 'possum up and brought it out to the table all on fire, but when the fire went out, the 'possum wasn't burnt at all. It was as good as it ever was which was pretty good considering that it was 'possum, not exactly our favorite critter for dinner. But in those days you got by on whatever you could.

The best thing that ma ever fixed, of course, was her Sunday-go-to meeting day, young springer, southern fried chicken. It'd pretty near melt in your mouth before you could eat it. It was so good. Next Sunday, Luther Gates was supposed to come over to eat Sunday dinner with Anna, so we'd be bound to have fried chicken then.

Well, Luther Gates did come over that next Sunday and we did have that delicious fried chicken. I got a leg and two thighs, 'cause those are my favorite pieces, and mashed potatoes, and gravy, and fresh green beans fresh out of the garden, and ma's hot buttered biscuits covered with sweet golden honey. Not bad eating for a poor country boy.

At dinner Luther made a startling announcement. He said that he was going with his Uncle John Henry on Monday to join up with the Confederate Army. We all just kinda dropped our mouths open for a minute. When the silence broke, Anna jumped up from the table a crying and ran outside on the porch. I guess she just couldn't take someone else she loved taking off to war and leaving her here all alone. Took her a good while to settle down, actually. It interrupted our dinner some but didn't stop Ben and me from getting another biscuit and some more honey. After all, we wished we were going too. This whole war was going to be over and we weren't even going to get to see any of it.

Luther loved Anna and Anna loved Luther. He said that when he came back he wanted to ask her hand in marriage, and that they would settle down on a little piece of land his father had set aside for him over on Noses Creek. "This is a tough time," he said, "and a man has to do what a man has to do." Just what did a man have to do I wondered to show that he was a man and not a "scared chicken shit" as some of the boys called some of the fellows. It was a man's world and soon we'd all have to show what we was made of, tough iron like two edged steel or just salt water taffy.

I reckon on Monday morning Luther and his uncle John Henry went on over to Powder Springs and got signed up with some of the Powder springs boys. There were several outfits that had been formed from that area. I'm not sure if they were able to join up with some of them or if they got joined up in some other regiment. By now you never knew 'cause a lot of the regiments were already looking for replacements.

Luther would do well though, for he was an easy going sort of guy who could get along with just about anybody. Now, his uncle John Henry was sort of rough and tough and didn't make friends real easy but he was a nice enough fellow. John Henry was big and burley, weighed about two hundred twenty five pounds and had a nice full beard and mustache. I knew him from holidays mostly, when some of the town people would get together for celebrations. Also, he was a pretty good friend of pa and helped out around the farm once in a great while, like when we were doing some stump blowing with black powder down on the bottom land near Gothards Creek. John Henry would make a fine looking soldier in uniform if they could find one big enough for him. Old Luther would look okay too, but they could probably put 'the whole of him down one pant leg he was so skinny and lean.

That Monday morning was a hard time as we thought about Luther and his uncle John Henry going off to war. Lots of boys had gone from around home already and more and more were leaving every day. Wasn't no end to it, it didn't seem. We heard that some of the armies were already way up into the thousands of men.

That was hard to imagine when you never saw more than a handful of people at a time anyway. One time I saw about three hundred fifty people at a fourth of July parade in Carrollton, Georgia, and I thought that was all the people in the world. To think in terms of fighting side by side along with a thousand men, and going up against another thousand men on the other side, now that was awesome. Somehow, I envied Luther and John Henry.

The days went on by slowly for a while. With little word from the front and not seeing too many folks anyway kept us a bit isolated down on the farm. Every day we'd be hoping for a letter or some word about pa, and Will, or Samuel and Levi. And now we were listening out for Luther and John Henry.

Summer came on and the roads began to get dusty from the lack of spring rains. June was always such a hot month anyway, but this year it seemed a little hotter a mite earlier. The crops really needed more rain. Everything in the garden was a starting to wilt down a little. Unless we got some rain soon, the garden and crops weren't going to do very well. But like ma says "some things you just can't do anything about, so you have to go on and accept them," Lack of rain, I guess, fell into that category.

Tomorrow would be boring again, I was afraid, and I didn't really expect anything out of the usual to happen. Just another quiet, dry, hot day on the farm. Maybe Ben and me would go swimming down at the pond or down on Sweetwater Creek at our old swimming hole. Yeah, that's what we'd do, go down to the old swimming hole and cool off.

The next day, that's exactly what we did. Anna stayed near the house with ma 'cause she wasn't as crazy about swimming as we were. It was Saturday anyway, and we always took most of Saturday off from work when we could. At least half a day in the afternoon, but this day we took off early for the creek. About mid morning. You've got to give the sun time to get up over the trees so as to dry you off when you get out of the water. I never did like to swim in the shade. Just wasn't right. Didn't feel right.

We had an old rope swing tied way up in a tree on the bank, and had even fixed a sort of a platform up on the big limb. We would climb up there and jump, swinging way out over the creek, and then drop loose. We thought this was the most exciting thing in the world to do. Most of the time the younger kids wouldn't climb up in the tree because it was too high. You had to be pretty brave to take such a big chance as that.

Splashing, and jumping and diving, we played nearly all the morning and into the early afternoon. There was half a dozen or more of us that had gathered at the creek that day from the surrounding farms. Some of the kids, like Ben and me, had brought some biscuits and sausages, and the like, from home. Everybody got kinda dried off and we found us a cool, dry place up under the trees to have our lunch. Ben and me were the oldest boys there, then there was Ty and Lonnie, about twelve and thirteen, from the Fraiser farm. And there was their two kid sisters, Joyce and Marilyn, who were identical twins, about ten years old. No skinny dipping today! Not with girls! So we left on our britches. And then there was Scott and Jeff Perryrnan, two brothers from over at the Perryman Farm, who were about nine and ten, respectively.

We had all become good friends over the years and had been swimming in this old swimming hole together for a long time. While we were eating our lunches and resting on the bank under the cool shade trees, we began to talk about the war up north in Virginia and up in Tennessee. It all seemed like a long ways off for us all on that warm summer day. Nearly all of us had older brothers, and fathers and uncles who had gone off to fight in the Confederate Army. Scott and Jeff's father had somehow got caught up in the Confederate Navy and had gotten assigned to some ship they called, "The Alabama". They said from the few letters they had received that their pa was doing real good and that they had already fought and sunk a number of other ships up and down the coast.

The Fraiser kids said their pa was in the artillery and had command of four big cannons in the 12th Georgia Light Artillery. Said in a letter that after the war was over he was going to bring home, each one of them, their very own cannon ball for a keepsake.

Ben and me told them about our pa and how he was in the cavalry with our horse Chester, and how they had fought at Shiloh Church and all. And we told them about our brothers Will, Samuel and Levi who had been at the battle of Bull Run Creek near

Washington, and how later they had been in some other battles up in Maryland and Virginia. They said they had even been as far up as West Virginia with the lst Georgia Volunteers Regiment.

We were all bragging, of course, about who was the best and who had done the most, Then too, we were awfully proud of our families and the contributions they were making to this war. To us it was all like a game of checkers.

CHAPTER 8

Too Close to Home

That summer we did learn of some very exciting news that had taken place practically right under our noses. Why, we had been invaded! The great state of Georgia had been invaded by Yankees ! Yankee spies actually, who had come down from up north to steal a railroad locomotive by the name of the General.

It had all taken place just about twenty-five miles north of our farm over at Big Shanty, Georgia. The train had been coming out of Marietta early that morning, and they had stopped over at the Lacy Hotel for their usual breakfast stop there at Big Shanty, just near Kennesaw Mountain. As a matter of fact, it was the next stop after Kennesaw Station.

While the engineer, and fireman, and conductor and other passengers had gone in to eat breakfast, a guy by the name of Andrews, and about twenty-one other men, spies, somehow took over the train and took off with it right up the tracks toward Chattanooga. "Unbelievable!" everyone said. Their objective it was said, was to destroy the key railroad bridges along the northern rail line and to disrupt and cut off the southern supply lines to the Confederates in Nashville. Also, such a raid was suppose to strike terror in the deep southern heartland of Georgia, as no enemy army had ventured into the south this deep. It was to show us just how vulnerable we were to the yankee critters.

Their plan was carried out with great precision, at first, and things looked pretty good for the Yankee invaders. But, they didn't count on a Mr. Fuller, the train conductor, who was determined to see that the General was caught up with. He and another man took off after them on foot until they found a pump car that they then took to chasing down the General. Steam locomotives were fast, but they still had to take on wood and water and Mr. Fuller knew that sooner or later he'd be able to buy some time in the chase.

Somewhere on up the line, Mr. Fuller intercepted another locomotive named the Texas. It was heading south and had been pulled over on a side track for the General to pass going north. Mr. Fuller commandeered the Texas and going backwards as fast as he could, pursued the General. It must have been one of the most exciting chases that ever took place! What, with all the smoke bellowing from the grinding and chugging locomotives a chasing each other up the long grade to Kingston and Dalton.

Those Andrew's Raiders, as they was later called, must have tried every trick in the book to stop Mr. Fuller and the Texas from catching up with them. The chase was so close that Andrews didn't hardly have time to tear up nothin' along the way. In the meantime, Mr. Fuller had been able to get off a telegram to Dalton, before the lines up there were cut, telling them the General had been stolen and to intercept them at all cost.

It wasn't too long until the Confederate Cavalry was closing in on the General. They had already tried setting some of the cars on fire and blocking the Texas and trying to wreck it. Didn't work though, and by the time the Confederate Cavalry caught them there was a shootout, and all the Yankee spies took off in different directions trying to get away.

Nearly everyone of them was captured eventually, along with Mr. Andrews, who was actually a civilian. They were all tried in a military court over in Atlanta and found guilty of treason and being spies. Except for some who later escaped, they were all hanged, including Andrews, down at the old jail house in Atlanta, and they were buried in Oakland Cemetery.

This was big news stuff, happening right here at home, practically within just a few miles of our home. It really made you stop and think about how close things were beginning to get, and it made you wonder if this would be about the end 0£ it or would this just be the beginning of a larger yankee invasion.

Most people said the south would never be invaded by the yankees. That they would never get this far down. There was a lot of ground and a lot of rebel soldiers between here and up north. But the Yankees did seem to be inching down the map a good bit. As long as they didn't come any farther maybe we'd be alright. Nothing can be as unsettling as a fox in the hen house. Out in the open, and on ground of our choosing, that was the way you wanted to fight a war. General Stonewall Jackson, 1 think, had once said something like that up in Virginia or somewhere.

Now, there was a soldier and a general of men! They said at the Battle of Bull Run: 'There stands Jackson and his men like a stone wall". Ever since then the nickname just stuck like honey to a biscuit. They said he was a very religious man, who often called on the almighty, and that he sorta kept to himself a lot.

All the men didn't necessarily like him that much, except they had a profound respect for him as a military leader and they would follow him anywhere, and anytime. We needed more leaders like old Stonewall.

The Confederate Army, about this time, was headed up by a general by the name of Albert Sydney Johnston, who President Jefferson Davis had a great deal of.:confidence in. He was an aggressive leader and fighter and was making good progress with the war when he was killed at the Battle of Shiloh Church. Quite a way to end a long and illustrious military career, which had began back in the Indian wars and the war for the, then, Republic of Texas, before it became a state. The loss of General Johnston was a serious loss for the Confederacy and would be felt for some time.

Johnston's replacement was a man by the name of Robert E. Lee. Lee was a simple man from Virginia, an educator, a military West Point graduate, and an officer in the United States Army at the outbreak of the war. As a matter of fact, before he resigned his position, he was personally offered the job of being commander of the United States Army, but he declined when his beloved state of

Virginia seceded from the Union. Fortunately, we got him on our side. General Robert E. Lee would prove to be a real "God send" to all our boys in gray.

The war was getting weary now. A good while had passed since Will, Samuel and Levi had first joined up, and then pa. The glory was fleeting very fast as news of the dead and wounded continued to come in from points allover the south and north. God must be watching over pa and the boys and protecting them from harms way.

Almost two years had passed now, and it all seemed like an eternity. Word from pa and the boys had been sparse and most of the news we got was from the newspapers and word of mouth. What would become of it all? Indeed, what would become of all of us?

CHAPTER 9

Loom and Gloom

No where, was the war more devastating than on the people staying back home. Left back home to survive on whatever remained available and with whomever was still there. The young, the old, the feeble, the disabled, women and girls of every age and description. Ma and Anna were no exceptions. They were certainly caught up in between things. Between family. Some had gone off to war. Some still here to look after. Luther Gates, Anna's sweetheart was gone to war, and she longed for him and worried for his safety. Ma worried continuously about pa and the boys and prayed for them every morning and every night.

One evening after supper, ma gathered us all around the table and cut us an extra piece of apple pie each, poured some more coffee, and said that she wanted to talk to us.

Ma said, "boys, I have an announcement to make concerning our future here and what I think our contribution should be to help end this terrible war. Anna and I have been talking. We've been talking seriously about the possibility of Anna and me putting in an application down at the New Manchester Mill. For almost two years now, the mill has been making Confederate uniforms for our armies and we know we can't shoot a gun, but we can sew and do something for our men here at home. Now, I don't know if they can use us right now, but I heard that they were a little short on help because of the war and all, and that they could probably use some extra hands.

My plans would be for me and Anna to walk back and forth to the mill at first and if it got to be too much, we'd see if we could get a room or something down at New Manchester. It's about six miles here from the farm and it wouldn't be too far, but we'll just have to see.

It would be you boy's responsibility to keep and maintain the farm and home here as best you can. You're old enough now and I think I can depend on you for that much. Now what do you think boys?"

For the longest time there was nothing but silence. Neither Ben or me was able to say a word. We were really dumbfounded! Could this be our ma and younger sister, saying all this and planning to do what we thought unthinkable. And here we were, almost two grown men, and doing nothing ourselves to perpetuate this national adventure and here were the women of our family fixin' to take off like they was soldiers themselves or something. And leave us here!? I don't think so.

Ben spoke up first and said, "Ma I guess you have to do what you think is the right thing to do. That's the way you have always taught us, and I know you have to follow your heart. And it's probably better that Anna go with you and you two stick together. Stevie and me will take care of the farm for right now until we can get signed up in the army."

"No!" ma said emphatically. "I can't have more of my boys and family committed to this war. Somebody has got to stay here and take care of our home. I just can't risk you and Stevie a taking off to join the army too. I won't have it, and you'll not do it except over my dead body, and that's final."

But ma!" Ben said. "I'm seventeen years old! In another year I can be conscripted anyway, and Stevie's sixteen almost."

"Yeah ma," I interjected. "We want to fight too. We want to be soldiers."

"I'll not hear of it, not another word" ma said. 'your job for now is to stay here and take care of this farm. Is that clearly understood by both of you ?"

We didn't say nothin'. We just sat there like two bumps on a log. A log that had just been whacked up side of the head with a mighty blow from a sharp ax. We respected our ma a lot. No, we reverenced our ma almost with the holiness that only the good Lord Himself, was really due. If ma said we would stay put, then we guessed we would stay put, at least for a little while. We would just have to see. Yeah, we would just have to wait and see. It was only a matter of time and we all knew it. Things would never be like they was before. Our family would never be back all together again. Things would be different. Very different. They had to be. They will be.

Two days later, Ben and me walked ma and Anna down to the New Manchester Manu£acturing Mill, taking with them a few things so that they could stay if somewhere was available.

The day was fair and clear when we started out. But by the time we traversed the six miles or so it had clouded up pretty bad. As a matter of fact, some thunderheads were rolling in and the sky was turning an ominous gray like the uniforms our brothers and pa were wearing. Like the gray yarn and wool and cotton cloth that ma and Anna would soon be making into Confederate uniforms.

The trees hung low over the winding road down and over Beaver Run Creek as we neared the approaching destination.

It wasn't long before we came upon the upper waters of Sweetwater Creek, the delivery system for tons of power captured by the fall of what everybody called, the factory shoals. Nearly a fifty foot drop in three hundred yards made for a wonderful set up for a moderately long mill run. It emptied through the water gate archway onto a massive 50,000 pound undershot water wheel. It was most impressive. As was the mass of the five stories above, reaching up out of the ground and climbing almost up to Heaven itself. It was truly an awesome sight to see something so massive and industrial buried away in the woodland on a creek side, 15 miles from Atlanta. People said it was the tallest building in the whole state of Georgia. I know that I had never seen any buildings this high in Atlanta before or anywhere else. It was truly magnificent; with its copper shield roof gleaming like a gold ring, even under the overcast sky.

As we neared upon the great factory we began to pass several people coming. and going on various errands and such. One kind lady, who was walking by herself, stopped for a minute and introduced herself, as Mary Ferguson, wife of Angus Ferguson, who had the grist mill just up the stream a ways. She was very nice, and said she had been down to the big mill to visit her sister, Martha, who helped in the company store. Mrs. Ferguson invited us all down to her husband's mill for dinner that evening if we could as they had built them a little house up near the mill and she longed for some women company to talk with. Ma told her how much we appreciated the invitation and that we would be more than happy to oblige. She passed on down the winding little road along the creek until she was out of sight in the bend of trees.

The water rushed down the mill race, as we raced along with it, ever closer to the industrial behemoth, which sucked up the water like a giant sloth and spit it out just as fast. The roar of the turning water wheel and the massive cranking and creaking of leather belts, and drives, and textile machinery brought new life to the otherwise barren sounds of the forest. And people too, not quite as noisy, were muttering around like ants clambering in and out of the massive man-made ant hill of brick and mortar.

It was not only a factory, but a true factory town, with houses of various types scattered over the surrounding hillsides, and a store or two thrown in to round out its mysterious ambiance. You couldn't see it all at one time because of the density of the forest. Massive trees hung low over the entire specter of the town, like they was trying to hide it all in a green foliage camouflage from the Yankee army, and indeed from all prying eyes. As we approached this land of mystery and intrigue, we made our way up to what was obviously the Company Store. Once inside, our eyes adjusted to the dim light and we could see an older, middle aged woman behind the counter putting something into a round tin.

"Hel-lo!" she said rather briskly as we stood there trying to take it all in and letting our eyes further adjust to the darkness of the interior.

New Manchester

"Can I help you?" she said.

"Yes," said ma. "My daughter and I are looking to make application to the mill for work."

"Ah ha," said the lady. "Well, what you'll have to do is go over to Mr. Cranbell's office over at the mill itself. It's on the second floor, just up the stairs over there, and he will be able to help you. I hear they are looking for a few replacement workers, especially since the war has taken a number of our able-bodied men."

"By the way," she said, "I'm Martha Jenkins, and you are?"

"Virginia Jett," my ma said, "but my friends call me Ginny, and this is my daughter Anna, and my sons Ben and Steve. Ma almost never introduced me as "Stevie" out in public anymore because she knew it sort of embarrassed me. She saved that for sort of a personal endearment now.

"Please to meet you," said Mrs. Jenkins.

"Yes, I think we met your sister, Mary Ferguson, on the road down to the mill here. She has been so kind as to invite us to dinner this evening."

"That's wonderful," Mrs. Jenkins said. "Maybe I'll see you at dinner. I nearly always eat with my sister and husband, now as my husband, Mr. Jenkins, is off fighting in the war, you know, like nearly every other man around here.

"Well, that would certainly be nice to see you this evening Mrs. Jenkins, we shall look forward to it."

"Oh, call me Martha, please. All my friends do. Lady friends, that is," she said with a sort of smirk and tickle.

"Okay Martha," ma said. "Well, we'll see you this evening and thank you very much for your kind assistance." And with that, Mrs. Jenkins nodded to the side and smiled as we turned and walked out the door, back into daylight once more.

Just across the road and up the way a bit, was the large factory with its staircase built onto the side. We'd have to enter there through this rather heavy door and ascend to the second floor to get to Mr. Cranbell's office.

The heavy door swung almost effortlessly, as though it was used a hundred times a day, and probably it was. The stairway was well lit from the natural light outside due to the windows all around it on three sides. As we began to climb the stairs, the old boards of the stair, worn smooth with use, and oiled for preservation, creaked softly and vainly as we marched upward. Sunlight, now breaking through the clouds, broke also through the windows of the thick walls and cast a beautiful warm glow across the wooden floor of the first landing as we turned to the next flight of steps. Upon reaching the second floor, we entered the closed door to the main part of' the factory and like a sudden rush of water, the noise from the working machinery suddenly gushed over us and inundated us with the magical sounds of massive machinery operating at full force and speed. It was a sound and sight like none we had ever seen or heard before in any of our lives. We were truly amazed and excited.

A few steps and we saw the sign for the Superintendent's Office and ma proceeded to knock on the door.

Come in the door is open," an older male voice hurled from the other side. ""What can I do for you?" said the short robust figure of a man in his middle fifties.

"Are you Mr. Cranbell?" said ma.

"Why yes I am ma'am, can I help you?"

"Mr. Cranbell, my name is Virginia Jett, and this is my daughter Anna and these are my two sons, Ben and Steve." Everyone nodded and greeted one another with a polite smile, but without words. Ma was the spokesperson here and she would do all the talking.

"Mr. Cranbell, we have come to make application here at the factory, that is, for me and my daughter Anna." My sons are going to return to our farm and care for it during our absence, and in the absence of their pa and three brothers, who are all off fighting for the Confederacy."

"Ooooh, good, Mrs. Jett, that's wonderful. Very commendable. We need every God fearing man who can bear a weapon right now." He takes a big sigh, like he just released an anxiety laden thought of tension. Like maybe we were going to win the war 'cause of our family was making such a monumental contribution to the war effort.

"We want to help make uniforms here at the mill for our boys. We're not exactly skilled in textile manufacturing, but we can both sew really good and we know how to use a loom. And, we're willing to learn anything we need to learn in order to do the job."

"Well, you know we don't pay much. Can't! Just isn't in the budget, but we do pay almost a fair wage. A dollar a day for you and the misses each, and you'll have to find your own room and board. Yes, I could use two good women in the loom room and the button room. Can you start right away? Say like, day after tomorrow? That'll be on Wednesday morning at 8:00 o' clock."

"Yes sir," said ma, "we'll be here."

"You can fill out your paper work then, Mrs. Jett, for you and your daughter Anna," said Mr. Cranbell.

"Thank you, very much Mr. Cranbell, we look forward to seeing you then sir" said ma.

Anna sort of curtsied and Ben and me shook Mr. Cranbell's hand to show our gratitude as well.

As we left the factory, and embarked back into the sunlight, which was now shining brightly in the mid afternoon, we decided to look around the town a little and see what was all there.

It was a peaceful town of about three hundred people, or thereabouts, with a good number of homes of all sizes and descriptions scattered over the surrounding hillsides. But, mostly the structures were built up on a big hill, just above the factory. The streets were little more than wide enough for the passage of two wagons abreast and were relatively unimproved. All dirt and all meandering like, here and there, up and down and around the hills and hollows around the mill. All, somewhat like a bunch of Indians hunkered down around a massive stone pot, from which brewed a mysterious life sustaining concoction of porridge.

That evening we did have our supper with Mr. and Mrs. Ferguson. Mary and her husband, Angus, were two of the nicest people you would ever want to meet. And, as she had said, Mary's sister Martha Jenkins, from the company store, was there as well.

We had a wonderful supper of beans and ham, sweet potatoes, grits and crisp cornbread, from freshly ground corn meal. All dripping in hot melting butter with all the fresh milk we could drink. It was out of this world. For dessert Mrs. Ferguson served little tea cakes, called funnels or something, with white sugar sprinkled all over the top and strawberry preserves on the top of that. Uuummm, uuuummm. We were in high cotton as they say.

During the meal, there was a lot of talk going on about nearly everything you can imagine, from the war, to new buttons they got in down at the mill, bright shiny brass buttons with the Georgia State Seal on them. Ma and Anna would probably be the ones to start sewing them onto the Confederate uniforms, as they had to be sewn on by hand and not by machine.

Everyone was concerned about the progress of the war. Mr. and Mrs. Ferguson had two sons who were off fighting in the war, who last time they wrote, were somewheres up in Maryland, according to their letters. A place called Antietam Creek in Sharpsburg, Maryland. Her boys were under the command of a General Longstreet. Mr. Ferguson said that they had been defending some kind of stone bridge over the creek and held the yankees off forever almost, when finally the lines broke and they lost the bridge. Eventually, General Lee was forced to retreat back over the Potomac River back into Virginia. According to Mr. Ferguson and the information he had picked up, this movement into Maryland had been a real effort by General Lee to gain Maryland recruits, pick up the European recognition and force the north to sue for some kind of peace settlement. But it just didn't quite work out that way.

The newspapers said a few days after the Battle at Sharpsburg, that President Lincoln had issued an emancipation of the slaves in all the slave holding states. According to the Fergusons, this was not going to go over well with our boys and it would just make them more determined to fight. But, then, on the other hand, it might make the northern soldiers more determined, as now they had more to fight for. Wouldn't hurt them anyway.

Tom and Harry, the two Ferguson boys, had also fought in some other battles called, Gains Mill and again at Mannassas Junction.

Ma said that Will, Samuel and Levi had mentioned some of those names in one or two of their letters. As far as we all knew, all the boys were alright and had not been wounded or killed in any of the action.

Mr. and Mrs. Ferguson said they heard a lot of news being there around the grist mill they operated on the upper banks of the Sweetwater Creek, just about a mile above the factory at New Manchester. They got the news from just about all the surrounding farms, as the families came in from time to time to get corn and wheat ground into flour and corn meal. Nearly everybody in the county had at least one or more family member off fighting in the war. And they knew and saw some of the other Miller families from time to time from the other mills like Maroney's, Alexander's, and Perkinson's. News traveled faster by mouth than it did in the newspapers. By the time something got reported and the papers got out into circulation and reached us, folks had already heard about most things, which were now in print.

At the supper table; Anna had told Martha Jenkins and Mr. and Mrs. Ferguson how her beau, Luther Gates was joined up too and that she had received two letters from him. That he, too, was somewhere up there in the Maryland and Virginia area and how he said that he had gotten himself wounded in the leg from a well placed bullet, but how it wasn't real bad and he was going to be able to save his leg. Thank God. She told them how she worried about Luther, day and night.

After supper, Mrs. Ferguson said we could all stay over at their place that night if we didn't mind some of us sleeping in the loft, in the barn or on the floor, but we'd do something. So we all figured how and where we were going to bed down for the night.

Martha Jenkins, during supper, had already invited ma and Anna, to stay with her at her nearly empty house down at New Manchester, since they would be working at the factory and had to have somewhere to live. She said she would really enjoy having the extra company and it would be good for all of 'em. So, that was settled and all would be taken care of.

The next morning after a hearty breakfast, ma and Anna left with Mrs. Jenkins to go on back down to New Manchester and Ben and I headed out for home. We had some chores to catch up on and a lot of thinking to do, as we pondered our part in this great under-taking. Somewhere, sometime, there must be a special place for us in all this adventure. We weren't about to live out our lives on the sidelines while the rest of the world just went a flying by like great flocks of Canadian geese. This time of year, they were heading south, but we knew for us, we'd be a heading north!

We would bide our time for a few months on the farm and get everything in the best order we could, and then around Christmas time we would tell ma and Anna. We would have to be as strong willed as ma or she wouldn't let us get away with it. It wasn't going to be so easy, not with nearly all the rest of the family already gone. On the other hand, maybe she would understand and give us her blessing, and we really did need that to take with us. It would be a long hard road ahead.

CHAPTER 10

Christmas at New Manchester

December 25, 1862, was a very special time in my life that year down in Georgia. It would be the last time, for a long while, that I would see my mother and sister Anna.

Ben and I had been talking a lot and we had decided to join up in the army ourselves right after Christmas. This would be our last family reunion for some time to come.

We had all been invited to come down to Mrs. Jenkins' house at New Manchester for Christmas so we could all be together, and Martha, as we called her, had invited Mary and Angus down to have Christmas dinner. It would be good to see them again, and to share news and conversation, and the joyous celebration of the birth of Jesus, our Lord and Savior. We didn't have much to give, but Ben and myself had been doing some special wood carvings to give as gifts and we were anxious to share these with our family and new friends.

As we made our way east down toward New Manchester a light snow began to fall early that Christmas morning. Maybe we'd have a white Christmas this year. Almost never did, 'cause the snow just didn't usually come until later in the winter. But, who knows, maybe it would come early this year. As we approached the large factory mill we could see the warm gray smoke of celebration from around fire hearths, softly rising up into the layered sky blanketing the cozy woodland

From nearly every home, Christmas smoke bellowed like pipe smoke heralding the beginning of something good and wonderful. Although the factory was operating on a half shift this day, the air of activity was everywhere. People were bustling up and down the small streets, going here and there, and there was definitely the excitement of a holiday permeating the cool North Georgia countryside.

The Company Store, where Martha worked was shut and locked up for the day as we passed by and noticed the big green wreath made from pine and cedar boughs gracing its door. On it was a big red ribbon and bow decorating the fresh evergreen. It was our first real sign of Christmas.

Making our way on up the hill and around the curve toward the summit, we noticed a fair amount of commotion going on. The mill factory itself hummed away with the bumping, grinding muffled sound of big machinery, which ran now day and night, except for very rare occasions, when there would be a break in the supply of materials coming out of Atlanta or from Alabama.

The house that Martha lived in was a two story, unpretentious type of boxed dwelling built like a square with a little front porch and a ridged, gabled roof, with a chimney in the middle. It too was pushing out gray smoke interrupted with burning cinders, a sure sign that someone had just poked up the fire. The house was a clap board siding and had never been painted. As a matter of fact, most all the houses and buildings had not been painted, but had conditioned themselves under the natural weathering of the elements to soft gray and earth tones of color. The chimneys were made from bricks, a rich red color from the natural red Georgia clay, fired only a few miles away at the brick yard at Salt Springs which had supplied most of the building brick for the factory itself. Between the colors of it all, the surrounding evergreen trees, good old Georgia pines and cedars, and the freshly fallen snow, created a sort of a surreal appearance, like one might see in some storybook. The white stuff continued for quite a while, but it would never accumulate enough for this Christmas to be considered really white.

Ben knocked on the door with his free hand and in just a minute the gate to Heaven swung open. Inside we were warmly greeted by Angus first and then Mary, his wife, and as we took off our overcoats and hats, Anna and ma came bursting in from the kitchen into the warm cozy receiving room, where a blazing yellow warm hot fire created an ambiance of warmth and safety. After warm hugs and kisses and all that good stuff, Angus came back in with a glass of wine for each of us. Now, we didn't drink, per se, but pa always said and ma did too, that a glass or two of libation was acceptable at special times like holidays and such. So, we accepted with profound gratitude. After everyone was served with their own individual glasses, Angus said that he wanted to make a toast.

"To the boys in gray, may they weather the storms and survive the fray, come home in victory and be safe today!"

"Hear, hear!" everyone joined in, in consensus of sentiment. We had a fine meal, a real kings treat, that day. We were indeed fortunate to have so many good cooks to spoil us men. We especially enjoyed the rich company and conversation. The fellow-ship of being with others who cared about you and who you cared about with all your heart. It was a happy, a wonderful and a joyous occasion that day at New Manchester in the home of Martha Jenkins.

The afternoon lingered on until—Dong, Dong, Dong, Dong, went the large bell from the factory belfry, signaling the four o'clock hour and the changing of the shifts. One shift off and another one on. The war effort had to go on, except this day, ma and Anna wouldn't have to go to work, as they were on the half shift that was off for Christmas. Normally, they would go on at four and work 'till midnight, when the graveyard shift came on. It wasn't uncommon at all for many of the workers to have to work double shifts. This day, this hour, we would have the rare leisure of family being together, and we would cherish the opportunity to bask in the love of family and friends.

After a while, it was time. Time we knew to tell ma and Anna, and Angus, and Mary, and Martha what our big decision was. Ben, being the oldest, delivered the foreboding news, and I reiterated nearly every word, so as to give greater confirmation and affirmation of our decision. I guess I sounded like some little sir echo, as we carefully made out our case for such an important decision.

At first, there was nothing but silence, then some crying by Anna and Martha. Angus just looked up and across at ma for some sign of acceptance, and Mary looked too, with some kind of face like, well, what can we all do?

Ma didn't say anything. She just stood up, turned and left the room and went back into the kitchen, raising her hand as she went, as she often did, as a sign not to bother her for a moment 'til she could regain her composure. The rest of us just sat there in the parlor for what seemed like an eternity, until Angus said, "Well boys, I for one am proud of you. You'll both make fine soldiers," he said in his characteristic Irish drawl. "Look out for Tom and Harry, will ya?"

About that time, ma re-entered the room and with her arms crossed she stood before us and said, "Ben and Stevie, as hard as it is for a mother to let go of her babies, you have my blessings." And she threw open her arms as a signal for us to draw near to her loving arms, so as she could grasp hold of the things she loved just one more time. To let us know just how very, very much we meant to her. And as we hugged our mother, Anna came up and joined in on the hugging and kissing, and then Mary and Martha had to join in, as well. All the while, Angus stood close by but maintained a manly distance until he too broke down and had to give us a proper Uncle Angus-like hug himself. "For the luck of the Irish," he said. By this time, we were all shedding a few tears." We all understood the gravity of the situation, but we each one knew in our hearts that there was no other way.

Ben and I left Martha's house that day knowing that we had made a man's decision, and now it was up to us to be the man we each thought we were. We knew that we were young, but we could hunt and shoot with the best of them, and in our hearts and minds, we knew we'd be good soldiers for the Confederate Army.

CHAPTER 11

Off To War

Ben and I secured the farm the best we could. No one would be around to take care of the animals so we turned the cows and hogs out to forage as well as the chickens. The cats and dogs would be on their own, too, but they had long ago learned how to forage off the land and around the farm. They would be alright. At least they would survive somehow.

In getting our things together, we figured we'd better travel light but take whatever we could to be as self-sufficient as possible. So we gathered up some blankets and various gear, like the old wooden canteens we had made and our cartridge boxes we had made ourselves in anticipation of becoming soldiers. Ben had a revolver he had acquired through trading and an old squirrel gun flint lock and we both had a few knives of various descriptions. Then it was time to take down grandpa's old shotgun, which was now my shotgun. Since giving it to me, my pa had been sure to leave it at home for 'some home protection and to get wild game with. Now it would become my main line of defense or offense with some blue bellied yankee. Maybe the army would have some standard issue rifles and equipment but we didn't know and it might be some time before we met up with the regular army.

Leaving the confines of our peaceful farm was a traumatic experience. Neither Ben nor myself, had ever left for such an extended purpose or indefinite time. As we looked back at the gate for one last look, we fought back the tears of sadness that we might never see our home again, but the excitement of adventure overcame our emotional farewell and we moved on down the road toward a new World and a new beginning.

Two days later we were in Atlanta, Georgia, the big city. The day was New Yearls Eve, December 31, 1862. It was an exciting time in an exciting place. The city was alive with activity, with Wagons and horses, and people going up and down every street in every direction. The air was clear and crisp, with an overcast sky and just a hint of snow hangin' in the cool breeze.

Ben and I had a little money with us that we had brought from home, and we decided that today we would have a fine dinner in a fine Atlanta restaurant and that we would celebrate the eve of the new year in style with the big city folks.

That evening was pretty Special as we sat down to dinner about six o'clock in the eating establishment of Herron's Restaurant, one of the finest in the city. We had a big order of special pot roast with candied yams, mashed potatoes, greens, corn and cranberry sauce and all the hot buttered biscuits we could eat. The young lady who waited on us was named Stephanie, as she had introduced herself when we sat down. She was a tall, slender, and beautiful young girl of just about our age with long blond hair put up in a bun. She was wearing a calico dress of burgundy and white with some frilly lace, ribbons and bows. She was a real pretty girl and her manners were perfectly matched in every way. We told her we were off to join the Confederate Army and this was our going away dinner so we really wanted to do it up right. She was so excited about our adventure she could hardly contain herself and said she would do everything she could to see that we had a goodtime and enjoyed ourselves every minute, and she did.

She kept our coffee hot and full and made sure we had anything and everything that we could possibly want. And for dessert, she even served us seconds on apple pie.

During the meal, Stephanie said that later that evening there was to be a New Year's Eve party at her father's home and she wanted us to be invited if we could come.

We told her we'd love to come and she gave us the address at 286 Peachtree Street. She said it was a big two story Victorian house at the corner of Marshall and Peachtree, and we couldn't miss it. There would be lots of people there from allover and we should have a very good time.

We were thrilled to have somewhere to go for New Year's Eve and to have met such a nice girl, as Stephanie, was a real added bonus. Who could know what new doors this evening's adventure would open for two country boys like us!

That night we arrived cautiously, not knowing really what to expect or how we might be received by almost total strangers, except for Stephanie that is.

The house was easy to find. It was probably the largest house anywhere around the area, although there was a number of large fine homes, the likes of which Ben and I had only seen from time to time. We had certainly never been in one like this before.

We made our way up the laid brick walkway under the cover of a light snow flurry. The wind was blowing now and rather cold, but the lights in the house made it look warm and inviting. And we could hear the merriment of people's voices and music emanating from within.

We ascended a few steps, walked across the wide veranda porch and boldly knocked on the front door. Within seconds the door was opened by a black man servant, a butler slave I'm sure, who said ever so graciously, "Yesss Sirrr, won't you come in please sirs."

"Yes, thank you, we are here to call on Miss Stephanie by her invitation."

"Yesss Sirrrs, I will fetch her for you gentlemen. Please be seated here in the hallway."

In just a few moments the negro man returned, followed by the most beautiful young lady in all of Atlanta, indeed, Georgia, itself.!

"Hellooo, Hellooo, how are you?" Stephanie said. "Did you have any trouble at all finding our home? I'm so happy you could make it! Do, Do come in!"

And before we could do very much more than just gasp, she was leading us away into the inner sanctum of the festivities.

"Thank you John" she said to the butler, as she took Ben by

the right arm with her left and lifting her skirt with her right hand we made our way down the grand hallway to the ballroom.

You could have put our whole house in that ballroom it was so big. The people were gathered all around in fine suits and dresses. Real southern ladies and fine well groomed southern gentlemen. We felt more like rag muffins ourselves but what we had on was the best we had and it would have to do. At least we were clean and presentable.

As we entered the large doorway of the ballroom, Stephanie called out loud for everyone to hear. "Ladies and Gentlemen!" she said as she grabbed me with her right arm, "I'd like to introduce you all to two new friends of the Confederate Army, Privates Benjamin and Steven Jett, off to the war effort; everybody make them feel welcome!"

And with that she turned and giggled with a girlish excitement like wasn't it just all so grand.

Ben said, "Well, Stephanie we really haven't gotten signed up yet."

"But we're going to first thing tomorrow!" I chirped in real quick.

"I know you will boys and I wanted to let everyone know what a fine thing you are doing, going off and fighting in the Confederate Army and all. It's a fine and noble thing!"

"Well, thank you Stephanie, we think we'll make good soldiers." I said to give reassurance to the idea.

"Come, come have some punch and cake and cookies and meet some of my friends." And we followed Stephanie, halfway dragging us across the large ballroom toward the punch table as the festive patrons all applauded us like they were sending us off to the war right then. It was certainly a memorable occasion for both of us. One thing we would long remember in the days to come.

At the party that evening we met nearly half of the population of the city of Atlanta, I think. Never, had either Ben or me met so many new people in one place. And they were all very nice to us. Just as cordial as ice cream to apple pie. And we fairly melted in the warmth of their enfoldment.

Stephanie, we found, had three sisters, Heather, Holly and Heidi. Heather was older by a few years and was married to a nice young man named Matt, whose family owned a local wholesale food brokerage business. It was from his family that Stephanie and Heather's father and mother bought most of the food for the fine restaurant they owned, "Herron's." Holly and Heidi were actually half sisters by a former marriage. Their mother had died some years ago due to some freak carriage accident with a train. They were even older than Heather and both of them were married and had several children of their own. Their husbands were both off in the army fighting for the South.

Stephanie's parents, Mr. and Mrs. Lucius D. Herron were both very pleasant to meet and seem to take an instant liking to both Ben and me. Mr. Herron was a bold, brash man with whiskers and mustache, slightly balding and more than slightly pot bellied. You could tell he was in the food business and loved it. He was jovial and had the greatest sense of humor. He insisted we stay through the fireworks and that we come again to visit his home and family.

Mrs. Herron was just as nice and cordial. She had the most southern elegance about her, as I think I have ever seen. She made sure that we had plenty to eat and that we had plenty of pink punch. Her countenance was most becoming to a lady of wealth and standing and her fine' jewelry she wore spoke wonders about the family fortune. They were indeed a wealthy family but their mannerism only showed a kind of gracious southern hospitality.

Just a while before midnight, I had the good fortune to meet another wonderful person, Stephanie's cousin, Debbie from Augusta, whose family was up in Atlanta visiting for the holidays. She was a very special girl who had long brown hair and big beautiful brown eyes and a figure to match. She was gentle and unassuming, but had a streak of vivaciousness in her that made her come alive with excitement at the least little thing. She would be the first love of my life. The first girl, yeah woman, to take my breath away with one full sweep. My heart went pitter-patter-flutter-flutter and I thought that I would not be able to contain myself for all the excitement I felt for this wonderful girl!

Debbie Langford and I watched the fireworks together that night over the snowy Atlanta skyline. Our hearts were joined as we held hands and marveled at the unfamiliar sights of blues and reds and greens, exploding and bursting overhead like giant epithets of love.

The party had been a God send to us in the midst of all this turmoil of war and strife. We would long remember the kindness we felt there and the warm personal relationships and friendships which were born that cold December evening.

That night the temperature fell even more and the snow crept in like on silent cat feet until by morning the whole of the country lay like a white virgin wool blanket across the Georgia landscape. Its beauty, unsurpassed and its whiteness unblemished by tracks or ruts. It indeed was a winter wonderland, one to be full of surprises and excitement for sure!

After a good, hearty, and late breakfast, at the little hotel we were staying at located on Whitehall Street, Ben and I figured we'd best be going on down to the local recruitment office, which was down on Alabama Street. So we did.

Upon entering the recruitment office, we were greeted by a Sergeant Lawson, who introduced himself, and said he was looking for a few good men this morning to start off the new year right. It was New Year's Day, January 1, 1863.

We told Sergeant Lawson we were there to sign up with the Ist Georgia Volunteers as our brothers were already in that outfit and we wanted to fight with them. He said that would be just fine and dandy but the Ist Georgia was already up in Virginia somewhere, he thought, in the Shenandoah Valley. What he needed were men for a new regiment being formed up called the 9th Georgia Light Artillery. We told him we didn't know nothin' about cannons and such and that we'd really like to be in the regular infantry along with our brothers up in Virginia. Well, he sort of scratched his head and said, "Well, look here boys, I can't really do much about putting you fellas up there with your brothers, but I'll tell you what, let's compromise. Say, I'll sign you up with the 9th Georgia Light Artillery, and iffin' and when you run up on your brothers and the Ist Georgia, you can put in for a transfer. Fair enough?"

I looked at Ben and Ben looked at me and we sort of nodded in agreement. After all, what else could we do? We couldn't stand around talking about joining the army and never do nothing. It was now or never.

"Where do we sign, Sergeant Lawson?" said Ben as we both moved closer to the table where the paper work was.

"Right here, gentlemen, just make or sign your name iffin' you can write

"Oh, we can write sir, and read too, and we're both pretty good in math!" I said.

"Gooood men, we need soldiers who are educated, in the artillery especially. It's sort of a higher branch of the service, you know," he said reassuredly.

"See the supply corporal over there and he'll fix you up with uniforms and such, and you'll need to report immediately out to Fort Walker on the edge of town to a Sergeant Masterson who is with the 9th. Can you remember that? Just in case, here are your orders you are to deliver to Sergeant Masterson. And good luck boys. God be with you both!" And he turned to some other paper work like he was real busy.

We were in the army now and we both looked pretty sharp in our new Confederate uniforms and kepi caps. We would be issued our weapons and some more gear out at Fort Walker we were told. So with a great deal of pride and our chests a bulging out, we made our way out on the edge of the city to Fort Walker, which had been built as part of the defense system for the City of Atlanta. As a matter of fact, work was always going on around the city building various defense works of all kinds, even though nobody thought that Atlanta would ever need them, it was just in case. Just basic military precaution we were told.

Fort Walker was without a doubt the most military of anything that Ben and I had ever seen. Uniformed soldiers were all over the place doing various tasks from walking guard duty to engineering to cooking. Some were working with cannons and the cannon placements and we figured that would be what we would be doing pretty soon. We asked the duty guard at the entrance which way we'd find the Georgia 9th Artillery and Sergeant Masterson. He gave us some general directions and set us on our way. Shortly we arrived at a special camp just on the other side of Fort Walker where the new regiment was forming up.

We found Sergeant Masterson drilling some soldiers around a piece of field artillery. He was barking out orders right and left and fairly near hollering every word that came out of his mouth. Ben looked at me and I looked at Ben, with that kind of look that said, "Do you think it's too late to get out of this?" But we both knew better and we moved on down the hill.

A light snow blanketed the ground from the night before and all around the men resembled rabbits jumping here and there. The whiteness of the snow only gave greater emphasis to the intense exercises going on with the cannons.

"So, Cannoneers you want to be, eh? said Sergeant Masterson. "Well, this is the place to be I'd say. Where you two from anyway?"

"Salt Springs, Georgia, just west of Atlanta." was Ben's reply. "We're farm boys" I said. "But we're here to fight."

"And fight you will lads, fight you will, eventually." said the Sergeant.

"We're being moved out in a few days up toward the Carolinas. You'll probably see plenty of fighting before we're through. Our destination is up in Virginia to meet up with General Lee." He leaned over, looked around to see if anybody was close by, and he half whispered, "we're getting ready £or a major invasion of the north. Yep. Going to make another move right on Washington, itself, or something."

Ben and I both made faces at each other and then smiled like, well alright!

Get your gear settled and tent assignment from the quartermaster and report back here when you're finished. We'll be here a while. Now, get movin'!"

We shuffled off through the snow and finally found the

quartermaster's headquarters. A Major Johnson signed us up and turned us over to a Corporal Delaney who gave us the standard issue of one tent for two men, two blankets, two canteens, two mess kits, and two Remington Zouve Rifles, 58 calibre, along with the appropriate cartridge boxes, 100 rounds of ammunition, and a tin box of percussion caps along with a cap box to go on our belt. We were also issued two haversacks, sort of cloth sacks for carrying our personal belongings.

"Sign here," said the Corporal. "You don't always get the rifles like this being in the artillery and all, but we just got this new shipment in and: the Major said go ahead and issue them out before some other outfit confiscates them all. "After all, the artillery can't fire the cannons all the time."

"Oh yeah! I almost forgot, here, take these bayonets and sheaths also, you might need them one day too," he said. "Also, here are some red arm and neck cuffs and red pant strips to indicate you are in the artillery. Sew them on as soon as you can and here's you a couple of 9s pins to indicate the 9th Georgia Light Artillery."

"Well, thank you very much," we both said. It was better than Christmas morning getting all this stuff. Ben and I were pretty excited as we made our way to the camp area and began to sort out our priorities about camp. First, we'd get our tent set up and sort of organize our personal equipment and examine our new weapons and so forth. We could hardly contain ourselves we were so excited about everything.

We got back to the field and reported to the Sergeant about noon time and the Company P we were in was just breaking up for the mid-day mess call.

"Just fall in with the rest of the company" barked the Sergeant. "You'll get your hands on the piece soon enough!"

We joined the other soldiers and enjoyed a good mess of beans and pork with some biscuits, not like ma's but still pretty good. While eating we began to meet some of the other fellas in the company and it was good to make some new friends. Fellow soldiers-in-arms. Boy, what more could you ask for! We were real proud of ourselves and felt like we were on the greatest adventure of our lives.

The afternoon was spent learning and drilling all about the "piece" as it was called. We would be working and firing a twelve-pounder cannon, which was capable of spitting out a twelve pound solid shot ball a total distance of about one mile. We could also fire canister, a mixture of grapeshot and shrapnel, or we could fire an exploding shell that carried a timed fuse, depending on the purpose of our objective.

Ben was given the job of rammer, while I was given the job of loader. The procedure went something like this. One man would swab the barrel with a wet swab, on the end of a rammer pole, to be sure that there was no live fire in the breach.

Then while another man held his thumb, wearing a leather thumb stall, it was called, over the breach hole to prevent the sucking in of air, another would place the one-pounder charge in the barrel mouth, another would ram it home to the breach, another, me, would set the projectile ball in the barrel mouth, another, the rammer, Ben, would drive it into the breach. Then the artillery man would prime the breach hole, either with powder or sometimes would use a friction primer called a lanyard placed in the hole, and the "piece" was ready to fire. At that point the corporal in charge, the aimer, would be responsible for setting the sights and elevation and would then give the artillery man the command to fire. He would then either light the breach primer powder with a match line, on the end of a sword usually, or pull the lanyard type friction primer, and BOOM! the cannon would fire. This was the general procedure and it took five men to do all these various tasks, at speed, and the piece commander to sight it for elevation and direction. With everyone doing just their special jobs a battery could get off about three rounds per minute maximum performance, after a lot of practice. And practice we did. Over and over and over. 0£ course, most of our drill was just dry firing but we did a right smart amount of actual firing so as to get use to the piece and practice accuracy of fire and procedure. During a battle, there would be no time to learn or to practice the Sergeant said. Our very lives and the lives of our men would be depending on how well we each knew and did our jobs, and of course we had to know how to interchange jobs as well, in case the need was to arise. In short, by the time we were through with our training, we would know everything there was to know about that cannon and we would know how to use it with deadly accuracy and precision. We were the Confederate Artillery Corps and we were proud.

We were under the command of a Colonel Meyers, who was a tall, lean man, with a full bushy red beard and mustache, a rather jovial commander who had a dry sense of humor and who loved his men. He also loved the military and seemed to have a great respect for every soldier. We were indeed, fortunate to have such a commander and we would do good on the field of battle. We each knew it in our hearts.

In about two weeks, we got our orders to move out. It was somewhere in the middle of January 1863. Ben and I had both written to ma and Anna and had told them what a fine unit we were in and that we were headed out for the front, wherever that was.

CHAPTER 12

The Front

Two more weeks passed as we traveled north through the snow, rain, sleet, hail, and even some beautiful sunshine. We had already made our way past Augusta, Georgia and Camden, South Carolina. Soon we would be passing over into North Carolina, the Tar Heel State. We were pretty excited seeing all this new country and places we had never been before.

We kept moving north, over mostly flat land, until within a few more weeks we were joining up with some other and larger forces. We were at sort of a staging point for meeting up with the others somewhere in North Carolina and we would soon begin to move in great force up through Virginia and across the Potomac River.

Some of the boys had been engaged in some light skirmishes along the way but nothing major. Mostly sharpshooters and occasionally some outlaying picket lines, but no major forces. Ben and I had not been shot at, at all, thank goodness, and by the same token, we had not fired upon the enemy up till this time.

Our first encounter with the enemy was in the wilderness of northern Virginia, at a place called Chancellorsville and Fredericksburg Maryland. It was there that we got our feet wet so to speak, as we, under the joint command of General Stonewall Jackson and General Robert E. Lee, pounded the enemy with long range artillery fire from a place known as Hazel Grove. Our collective actions there brought southern victory but at some considerable costs. At places like Mary's Heights and the sunken road there was a great loss of life and it became known as the Second Battle of

Fredericksburg, somewhat like the first back in December of 1862. But this time we lost another great commander, when General Stonewall Jackson, was mistaken for the enemy upon returning to the southern lines, and he was shot by one of his own men it is said. He loss an arm as a result of his wound and within ten days later contracted pneumonia and died. He was a great leader and it was said that General Lee himself grieved deeply over his unfortunate demise. He even said if it could have been him he would have traded places.

Now we had fired upon the enemy and we had taken our place in battle, from a distance, as good artillery always likes to do if possible. But we hadn't seen the "Elephant", as they say. We hadn't exactly looked death in the face yet. Perhaps our time would come. Colonel Meyers and Sergeant Masterson were proud of our actions thus far and said we had done a commendable job and to keep up the good work. That made us feel better and we were anxious to contribute even more to the war effort as soon as we could.

In Virginia, we had become a part of the army under the direct command of General Robert E. Lee and would become a small segment of the large invasion force to invade and assault the northern states of Maryland, Pennsylvania, and New York, perhaps. We had even heard that we might even take Washington, D. C., either going or coming back. Generally we would stay toward the inland and away from major population areas like Boston, Baltimore, New York City and others along the Atlantic coastline.

There was even talk that if we did go with our invasion in the north, many southern sympathizers, like in Maryland, would probably turn to the south and secede, giving the Confederacy a great big boost toward victory with all the addi tional soldiers we might gain. The Lord knows we need every available man we can get to fight the yankees. We were still badly outnumbered, but for some reason the Federal Army didn't really take advantage of their superior numbers in force. I guess they really did agree that it took ten yankees to equal one good Johnny Reb. And nearly all the statistics backed up this premise. There was a certain conservatism about the Federal Army, like they weren't going to fight unless they absolutely had to, and everything, and every advantage was on their side. Maybe it wasn't such a bad strategy.

For months now, we had been gathering up and moving northerly into the enemy territory. We had encountered little or no resistance from the local population, although they were mighty surprised to see an invading army of so many upon their own home soil. Resistance was only token, as nobody really knew where the main force of the Federal Army was. It probably was somewhere around the area but we just didn't know. And apparently they didn't know where we were or they would have been on our tail like a duck on a June bug, at least I thought.

General Jeb Stuart's Cavalry, was the eyes of this great army, and he and his men were busy running circles around the Federal Army, apparently trying to embarrass it into surrender by mere intimidation. Word had it that if he could just go around them a few more times the yankees would fall over dead in the deep ruts made by General Stuart's Calvary.

But it seems that General Lee hadn't heard from General Stuart in several days and everybody was somewhat in the dark about general maneuvers and positions.

Seminary Ridge, Gettysburg

In the meantime we kept working our way on down the roads of Pennsylvania heading north. The countryside was beautiful and green and reminded me a lot about how my own homeland looked this time of year. Right at the end of June it was beginning to get a little warm during the heat of the days and the days were long with a lot of daylight from dawn to dust. We were making good time and the weather was fairly good and dry.

I'll never forget that morning of July 1, 1863, we were making our way down the pike toward some little Pennsylvania town called Gettysburg, when we began to hear the fire of muskets and a little later the undisputable sound of field artillery. North or South, we weren't sure yet, but we knew it wasn't us 'cause we were still moving forward in the column.

It wasn't long, probably an hour later, that we got our orders to advance rapidly, so as to deploy our artillery on a relatively high ridge just westerly and south of the hamlet of Gettysburg, called Seminary Ridge. It was called so, because of the old Theological School that was located upon it. It offered a supreme view of the underlying countryside to the east and would be a good place to position our artillery. within a short time the 9th Georgia Light Artillery was in position and ready to fire when commanded. The enemy had been intercepted on the right somehow and it was our orders to place a long range barrage toward the opposite ridge and valley as soon as the enemy could be sufficiently located and identified. Somewhere around mid morning we began to let them fly at maximum range about a mile over. We were firing on a line of dismounted cavalry which had been formed so as to fire on a column of Confederate Infantry, which had soon broken ranks and was engaging the enemy. It didn't appear to be a very strong force of Federals, maybe just one regiment or two perhaps but still that constituted probably a thousand soldiers or more. Unless they received reinforcements, they wouldn't be able to hold that line for very long. What we didn't know, that this was just the tip of the iceberg and only represented the long extended arm of the Federal Army.

For several hours we bombarded the Federal position until it became obvious that reinforcements were beginning to arrive. The line was strengthened and extended and eventually the Federals even brought up a Federal Battery and placed it in the wheat field opposite our lines. It appeared that they would try to blast us out of our position among other things.

Pretty soon here it came right over our heads, solid shot and exploding shells. We would soon be taking some direct hits if we didn't knock out that battery. It was pretty different now being the ones shot at by artillery and we weren't exactly happy about it. Colonel Meyers redirected our fire to the immediately assaulting Federal battery before us and said we would have to take it out before it took us out. within minutes we were redirecting our fire, laying into that battery everything we had but using mostly exploding shells. We must have taken and delivered perhaps a hundred rounds each way doing only minor damage to each others positions, when darkness began to fall and suddenly everything just stopped on both sides. The dead and wounded were scattered over the area and it was customary to use the twilight time to care for the wounded.

As for us; we had lost one man dead in Company A, and four wounded. One artillery piece out of four in our battery had been disabled and we would have to work into the night to restore its utility if we could.

By nightfall campfires began to be seen allover the area and it became obvious that this would more than likely really turn into a major engagement before it was all over.

As Ben and I got something to eat from the mess tent we took our plates and sat down under the stars and looked up at the great heavens above. We talked and wondered out loud about the world and how God must be looking down on all of us and wondering himself what in the world we were all doing down here, fighting and killing one another. We had even heard by rumor that some of the Federal batteries on the opposite side were commanded by a General Ayres from New York state, who we were sure was related to us back on our mother's side of the family. We had heard of him being a military career man but we had never met him and we really didn't know him, just the fact that he was probably kin folk and that sort of gave you a funny feeling. I guess if we never saw him in person we couldn't be too related. But that was the way this war was. There were actually brothers fighting against their own brothers in this war and probably right here in this battle. Sometimes fathers against sons and certainly uncles against nephews, and the such. It was a crazy mixed up war I'd have to say. The likes of which we had never seen.

The next morning we were up bright and early and the cracking of gunfire soon commenced with the early sun. This would really be a day to remember as lines on both sides began to form up and new positions were taken. From where we could see, the Federal line extended far to the right including a little mole hill of a mountain sort of which was called Little Round Top. It was the end of the line for the Federals, but why they didn't occupy the higher and bigger hill to their left is beyond my understanding. It would have most definitely given them a superior position over our assaulting lines; however, the implications of such strategy would only be known later.

While we began to blast the Federal lines to the east, an assault of Confederates under the command of McLaws began to advance upon the valley below. They made their way through a wheat field and a peach orchard and some of the most fierst fighting we had ever witnessed. Along the way they captured a Federal Battery. They then moved forward and the extreme right £lank moved through a real rocky knoll area at the base of the Little Round Top Hill. This rocky knoll area would later be known as the Devil's Den because the fighting there was so ugly and bad. Thank God that Ben and I were not down there and having to go through that awful hellish sight just before our eyes.

As we kept our bombardment up, the ground fighting kept going on throughout the day until our boys began to make frontal assaults up the slope of the Little Round Top. It was some real fighting going on and it appeared that it was only a matter of time before we took that hill. But the yankees were as stubborn as hornets and just wouldn't give an inch. So finally, in one big flanking movement the Confederate line swept up the far right of the slope in an effort to out flank the Federal line, but just as our boys reached the upper part of the slope, they were met by a down sweeping Federal bayonet charge, which effectively disrupted the assault and saved their line. It was some God awful fighting and both sides lost a lot of men.

While all of this was going on there was more fighting all down the line extending all the way down to Gettysburg and around a place called Culp's Hill, where the fighting had been equally dramatic and deadly this day. It also included, appropriately, a place called Cemetery Hill, there on the outskirts of town. By nightfall both Federal flanks had been thoroughly assaulted as commanded by General Lee, who wasn't about to let the enemy get away without being engaged.

By the next day a plan was on for an even more dramatic assault on the center of the Federal line, to be centered or focused around a small clump of trees along a stone wall. The ground to be covered would be almost a mile of open terrain and would constitute one of the most dramatic military charges of infantry in the history of the world, with approximately 15,000 men participating in the singular assault.

By this time our batteries had been repositioned and it would be our duty to lay a heavy barrage of long range fire upon the enemy line toward the center to cause as much damage as possible. Then, at the appropriate time we would be directed to give support and cover to our assaulting infantry as they made their way across the great gulf of space between us. Well, we did just that, and we fired practically every ball and exploding shell we had in our caisson's supply wagons. There was insufficient time to bring up our reserve supply wagons, so the assault would have to begin immediately to support the momentum of the effort. During the same time the Federal line was being constantly reinforced and re-supplied with both men and munitions. The Federal batteries were beginning to be a dreadful thing to deal with also, as they seemed to be constantly replaced even when knocked out.

The time came and, under the direct command of General Lee, General Longstreet had placed General George Pickett in command of three divisions—two of which were A. P. Hill's Corps—and the assault began, which would forever henceforth be known as the famous Pickett's Charge. Undoubtedly one of the most awe-inspiring military undertaking in history.

We kept up the long range cover for our boys for as long as we safely could and then basically our job was done. It was all we could do for the gray line as it made its way wave after wave after wave into the conflagration of battle before them, facing head on into exploding shells, thousands of musketry fire and cannon canister at point blank range. As we watched in wonder and disbelief we finally saw our battle banner briefly cross the stone wall precipice and rise triumphantly into the smoky sky. Then, almost as suddenly as it ascended, it came down and within a few minutes the Stars and Stripes was up again waving at us in angry defiance and our boys began to fall back. At least what was left of them. Falling back in a slow line of receding gray, much like the giant wave that crashes on the beach, spraying its foam in the air, then reluctantly draws away from the extremity achieved by the surging effort.

It appeared, there would be no battle tomorrow or the next day, as we had depleted and exhausted our resources in both men and fire power over these past three days. Three days that would go down in history as being especially awesome and deadly in the loss of human life and spirit. Some 53,000 brave men wounded and dead. How unbelievable, and yet how true. Almost immediately we began our preparations for a withdrawal to the south and over the next few days and weeks we moved south without ceasing until we had once again crossed the Potomac River and entered Virginia. We were getting tired and somewhat ragged, but we kept our spirits up and we were still ready, willing and able to fight and we would fight again another time.

CHAPTER 13

The Long March Home

It rained for the next two weeks, as we made our way south toward home and familiar ground. The cannon and caissons and supply wagons bogged down deep in the soft black and gray mud of Virginia. A rich and handsome, soil unlike the red clay of my native north Georgia. But mud was mud no matter how you looked at it, no matter how much you admired its richness, no matter how much you despised its stubborn uselessness. Mud was mud and we had plenty of it. Ever so often, we'd have to take poles we had cut and just knocked the caked mud out from between the spokes so we could keep moving. It was a toilsome retreat, especially under the extreme circumstances of defeat and loss.

Finally the rains let up and the sunshine broke through bringing warmth and refreshment to our rain soaked bodies, clothes and equipment. Somewhere along the way we also regained our composure and complete self confidence, as we knew this war was far from over. Our big opportunity to defeat the north on their own ground had failed and we would have to accomplish victory another way, probably on our own home soil.

A few days rest came as we made camp temporarily and attempted to put back together all the pieces of our broken regiments. New plans were being made and new strategies for war were smoking in the air along with the crisp smell of a side of bacon cooking for breakfast. It would be the first time in weeks we had eaten cooked food and it sure was good.

After breakfast, mail call arrived and with the usual whooping and hollering that goes along with a rare rejoicement of renewing old contacts and relationships with home and loved ones.

"Steven Jett!" the Quartermaster called as he flung a flying piece of paper toward where I was perched up on this log listening to the long litany of names never expecting to hear mine at all. I was there mostly for entertainment, just something different to do. Nobody hardly had been writing to me or Ben, except two letters we did get from ma and Anna back in the spring. Who could this letter be from? I wondered as I swooped down like a chicken hawk to fetch it almost before it hit the ground.

The address was just Steven Jett, 9th Georgia Light Artillery, Army of Northern Virginia. I examined every word as it looked so official and was written in the most beautiful Spenserian* hand writing I had ever seen.

Carefully I opened the envelope up to reveal its contents and it read as follows:

> My Dearest Steven, May 15, 1863
>
> I just had to write to you because I have been so worried about you and your brother Ben. So many boys have been killed or wounded since I first met you at my cousins' house in Atlanta. By the way, Stephanie is doing fine and her family is all in good health, except her father has been considerably overworked keeping adequate food and supplies for the restaurant, what with the war going on and all. Everything is begining to get a little scarce with the war demanding so much, but we understand. Even here in Augusta things are a mite tight.
>
> Steven, I hope you are doing well and have not had any trouble with so many of the things of war. I know there are so many hardships and circumstances over which you have so little control. But I also know that your 11 always be

* An artistic handwriting of the period and time widely taught in the schools, characterized by flowing lines and beautiful curves.

brave and face whatever you have to, like the fine soldier I know you have become.

I have really missed you and never did I realize that I could miss someone so much as you. I never believed in love at first sight but in your case I might be able to make an exception. I hope you don't think I am being too forward but I have enclosed a lock of my hair for you to carry with you in hope that you will remember me and know that someone is thinking about you. If you come by Augusta, maybe you can get a furlough to come and visit me and my family.

Well good-bye for now and be sure to tell Ben hello for me and that he can come too.

Love,
Debbie Langford
118 Savannah Street
Augusta, Georgia

As I pulled out the shiny lock of beautiful brown hair it glistened in the morning sunlight and beckoned my heart from some far off place to draw near and be comforted. Nobody had ever sent me a lock of their hair before, much less a beautiful girl who seemed to really like me, maybe even love me. She did sign her letter "Love" Debbie Langford. Maybe all girls wrote like that to fellas off in the war just to make them feel good. Oh well, it didn't matter;' because it worked. I did feel better. As a matter of fact, I felt great and I couldn't wait to tell Ben and to show him the beautiful and mysterious lock of brown hair she had sent to me.

Occasionally, along the way, we heard at various times by letter, from Ma and Anna back at New Manchester. They were doing fine and working in the mill every day making mostly Confederate uniforms and some shirts and trousers. Sometimes they would make socks, it just depended on their particular stock orders. Ma did say that Mr. and Mrs. Ferguson and her sister Martha Jenkins were doing fine and that Martha was still running the company store. A few more people had moved into the settlement as the mill had put on some extra shifts to meet the war demands. Mr. Cranbell ran a tight ship there at the mill and was a good Superintendent, mother said in her letter. Also a Mr. Henry Lovern, who was her immediate supervisor and Anna's was a good man with a good sense of humor and it made the life and work there more bearable under the hardships they were experiencing.

Mother had heard from Pa only twice by letter since he had left for the war, but he was doing fine at last count and was still riding with General Wheeler's Cavalry. Chester, Pa's horse had been shot out from under him and killed in a skirmish in Mississippi, called Brice's Cross Roads. Pa got a bad saber cut on his left arm but it had been healing real good and was almost as good as new by now. Of course, he had to be issued another horse and it never was as good as Chester but it was better than walking all over the country.

Ma also had heard from William, Samuel and Levi who had been all over the place with the Salt Springs Regulars and the First Georgia Volunteers. She thought they might have even been up in Virginia, maybe even in West Virginia in the Shenandoah Valley with General Stonewall Jackson's Army. According to their letters, they had all seen plenty of action and Will had been promoted to a Captain and was working in the Medical Corp in some capacity. He had told her how much pain and suffering he had seen in the field and how arms and legs were amputated with regularity among the wounded. Ben and I knew this was true because we had seen a good bit ourselves. Everybody knew if you got wounded it could easily cost you an arm or a leg, but if you got gut shot there was a better than good chance that you wouldn't survive.

Samuel and Levi had, been in some pretty thick action and Levi had a mini ball graze the top of his head during one battle. Blew his slouch hat right off his head and liked to have killed him, but it didn't. Samuel had burned his hands pretty bad on some hot rifle barrels during one engagement, and some artillery blasts had given him a concussion and knocked him out for a while but he was okay after a few hours. They thought he was dead, but he hadn't even been touched, just knocked unconscious for a while.

Ma and Anna prayed for us all as she figured that was all they could do was to pray and trust in the good Lord to take care of us boys and Pa.

Anna had heard some distressing news concerning her beau Luther Gates and his uncle John Henry. Seems that they were both crossing some creek up in Tennessee when their regiment was ambushed by the Yankees. Before they could get across to the other side a good number of soldiers were shot and killed including Luther and his uncle, John Henry. They never had a fighting chance under the circumstances. Anna, of course, was grief stricken and it was all she could do to go on knowing that she would never hear Luther's kind voice again or his beautiful banjo music. They had planned to marry sometime after the war. Now all that was changed and she'd never see Luther again. These were some sad times and nearly every family was affected in some way. I felt sorry for Anna and my heart grieved for her but that was all I could do.

News had finally reached the Army of Northern Virginia that Vicksburg had fallen sometime around the 3rd of July just about the same time as Gettysburg. Vicksburg had been under siege for a long time by the Yankees under the command of a General Ulysses S. Grant and a General Sherman. The fall of Vicksburg was a mighty blow to the Confederacy, as it was a real Key to the Mississippi River. But everyone suspected that after the fall of Fort Henry and Fort Donaldson, it was only a matter of time before Vicksburg would be surrendered. After all, it had been under siege for over six months and the civilian population was living on roots, rats and whatever could be scrounged up for food. They were living in holes in the ground like gophers and mostly coming out only at night to get some fresh air from the constant bombardment of siege artillery. Maybe it was a blessing to them that now it was all over except for the Federal occupation, which couldn't have been any worse than what they had already experienced. But you know it was humiliating for them. After all, the "South" was a proud people and southerners would endure Hell itself if that's what it took to defeat the Yankee army. And often times it was.

It was now mid Fall and we arrived in Augusta, Georgia, in anticipation of making a winter camp if possible. Perhaps while here I would be able to get a furlough and visit Debbie Langford and her family. I sure did hope so. Ben and I both needed some time off and some sort of refreshment from the drudgeries of war and being constantly on the move.

CHAPTER 14

Augusta The Wonderful

Ben and I both obtained a three day furlough while we were in Augusta, Georgia. The weather was better now and we were experiencing a few days of relatively warm temperatures. It was a welcome relief from having so much foul weather for so long. We just hoped it would last during our furlough so we could enjoy ourselves.

Augusta was a fair size city, being on the Savannah River just up a ways from the port city of Savannah, Georgia, where many goods and war supplies were always coming and going. Even as far up as Augusta, the shipping was pretty heavy. It was a well-founded city of about the size of Atlanta and we felt fairly comfortable in finding our way around. We decided that we would stick together as much as possible and that we would go look up Debbie Langford and her family first thing.

We asked some directions and soon found our way to 118 Savannah Street. The house that bore that address was rather large and somewhat pretentious looking and we were not sure that we looked presentable enough to announce our arrival. Nevertheless, we made up our minds to go on and we walked up the walk to the large polished door and rapped the brass knocker sending a sharp metallic sound resonating to the inside. There was no response for some time so we tried again. Still no response. We waited, anxious that either we might be turned away, or on the other hand, that no one was at home. The time was mid morning and we finally determined no one was coming to the front door, so we went around to the back of the house where we soon discovered a negro woman of middle age who was just commencing to pluck a chicken. She had obviously just rung its neck.

Augusta Fire Wagon

"Whatch ya'll want thar?'! she said, startled-like at our sudden appearance.

"Well mam, we're here to pay our respects to Miss Debbie Langford and her family."

"She ain't here. Ain't been here for two weeks now. Her folks neither. Gone up to Atlanta to visit kin folks. Who are you boys anyhows?"

We told her who we were and how we had come to know Miss Debbie and all, and how I had got a letter from her while up in Virginia.

"Oh, I sees" said the woman. "Well, thats most likely where's they are right now, up in Atlanta. I's just get tin' this here chicken ready to boil up for dinner tonight. Don't know whens they'll be back really, maybe this week, maybe next."

"Would ya tell miss Debbie we came by to see her and would ya give her this here whistle I carved out of a stick for her?" It was all I had, but I wanted to leave something for her to let her know we had really been there to see her.

"Yessire, I sho' would be glad to sir," and with that, she took the whistle in her hand and drew it up to her face to examine it more closely. I sure hoped she wasn't going to blow on it to see if it worked or not. When she saw my apprehension at her more than casual interest, she quickly lowered it back down and slowly put it in her apron pocket.

"Yessir, I's be glad to give it to her, I sure will," she said even more reassuredly.

We told her we would be around town for a few days and maybe we'd get a chance to check back with her, then we told her good-bye.

Now we had three days to do nothing it seemed. So we made our way down Main Street to see the sights and sounds of the big city and there were many. Just as we began to relax a little, here come this racing team of fire wagon horses followed by the craziest looking fire wagon you ever did see. It was ringing its bell to beat the band, with four razzled, dazzled old men barely hanging on for dear life as they rounded a corner on to the main street and headed down the street right toward us as fast as they could go, throwing up dust in a great bellowing cloud the size of Texas. It was all we could do to scramble out of the street and onto the wooden side walk, barely escaping with our lives. Turning and watching in disbelief, we watched the horses and wagon with the clinging men make a sliding turn again into the next street to the right. The bell was still clanging as fast as the fire-wagon was going and the dust continued to rise like it was caught up in a great whirlwind. By now we could see smoke coming up into the pure blue sky, what looked like, maybe two or three blocks away.

We decided, hey, why not, with that kind of look that only brothers can have without really saying anything out loud, and with that we took off after the storming fire quencher as fast as we could go. After all, maybe we could be of some help in putting the fire out.

When we got there we could see that it was a two story building already totally engulfed in flames. The men with the pumper began to dowse the flames with water but it was more like throwing grease on a pan fire. It only sizzled and looked like it made the flames spread out more and higher.

We helped form a bucket brigade from one of the watering troughs and threw all the water we could on that fire, mainly in an effort, I think, to try and save the adjoining buildings, 'cause we sure wasn't going to be able to save this one.

After everybody worked with the fire for about two hours, we all stopped and let the last part of the fire take the rest of its toll, while we began to really survey the damage that had been inflicted. Even our artillery couldn't have destroyed a building like this fire did, so completely and so effortlessly. Just "poof" almost and it was nothing but ashes when it finished.

After the fire, we found out the building that had just burned was an apothecary that had long served the west side of town. That, had probably explained some of what seemed like chemical explosions occurring during the fire.

We hadn't counted on the extra excitement with the fire and all but it was right down our alley, literally, and we took advantage of all the, well I almost said "fun", but I mean the excitement of the terrible fire. Yea. You know what I mean.

The afternoon moved on quickly because of the fire and we soon found ourselves getting somewhat hungry. It was already late afternoon and we figured we'd just have an early supper. We had just a little money, not much, but probably enough to eat on a few times, so we found this tiny little cafe that served up hot meals and we proceeded to make real pigs out of ourselves until we were so full we could hardly move.

Friday night it was, and there was bound to be some entertainment in this tin horn town and we were going to find it. As it worked out, we discovered a theatre and found out that some kind of Shakespearian play was about to begin just that evening. Romeo and Juliet, it was billed.

We paid our two cents per head and took the best seats in the house we could find down next to the piano. For two hours we watched and listened, and watched and listened some more, and watched and listened some more. Finally, the final curtain came down and we were able to get up and leave. It had been pretty good, especially for us country boys, who had never seen such a play, even though we were familiar with the story. The lady who played Juliet was magnificent, if not a little old for a fourteen year old girl. Nevertheless, she brought off her part with perfect credibility until she was supposed to be lying there dead and she kept coughing, once even rising to an upright position and then lying back down to be dead again. All in all, it was high class entertainment.

After a good nights sleep in a real bed in the local hotel, we were in no hurry to vacate the fine feather bed we had collapsed into, so we slept until about 9:00 o'clock. The whole day of Saturday was before us and we were anxious to make new discoveries in our new found town of Augusta.

After breakfast, we walked around the town for a while here and there and by late afternoon happened upon a little bar saloon, where we were tempted to sit down and have a couple of drinks. We were very tempted. In fact, we were so tempted that we actually did sit down and before I knew what had happened, Ben said, "We'll have two whiskies please." When they came, I wasn't sure to sip on it, swallow it whole, or get up and run out the door before I did something I was sure to regret. Following Ben's lead I decided to sip it at first. After a few sips and a few twisted expressions, we both decided there was only one way to handle a shot of whiskey and that was to wolf it down all at once in one smoothhhhh swallow, like a man was suppose to. After three more we were getting pretty good. And we were getting pretty mellowed out as the afternoon moved on into the twilight.

It was about that time when the women came down the stairs and made their way into, across and through the saloon, each finding their own particular roosting spots among the spar patrons at the tables and at the bar.

One of the girls was especially beautiful. In fact, I know she wasn't a girl at all, but rather a very sophisticated woman of the world who took a position on a stool at the bar, alone for the moment, apparently buying her last few moments of freedom for the evening. You could tell she was a woman tormented by her own beauty, torn between the lust of men and the sanctity of her own inner soul. As she turned slightly and surveyed the room with her wondering eyes; she stopped momentarily when she spied me and Ben sitting at our table half-way across the room. For a moment our eyes met and we both smiled as people do sometimes, like when you pass each other on the street and you don't really know each other, but you sort of wished you did. But there wasn't time for that, or was there?

The piano player had moved to the instrument and was beginning to plank out soft love tunes of some kind that Ben and I had never heard before. After a few numbers, the lady in the pale blue dress at the bar turned and left the counter, and carrying her drink, she strolled with all the ease of a gliding lark over to our table, where, when arriving, said "Hello boys, where yall from?" in the sweetest, softest voice I had ever heard.

We introduced ourselves and told her where we were from and so forth.

"My name is Gwendolyn, may I sit down?" she said.

"Why yes, yes you can Gwendolyn," we both said, half falling all over ourselves as we both jumped up to help her with her chair.

"You know this is a mighty big town fellas!"

"Yeah we know, we've been exploring around town some while we are off on our furlough," I said in a very matter of fact sort of fashion.

"Found anything interesting?" she said in her sultry voice.

"Well, yes, as a matter of fact we have," said Ben.

"Just yesterday we helped put out a fire down on Farley Street at the Apothacary."

"Do you think you might want to put out a fire tonight?" came her reply. "Well . . . I don't know," Ben said as he looked over at me with eyes as big as saucers.

"Do we want to put out any fires tonight brother?" he asked while trying to reach for the bottle and get another drink.

"Can we offer you a drink Gwendolyn?" I said.

"Just call me Gwen, all my friends do Steve," she said as she touched my right arm with her left hand which she left resting there for me to feel the pulse of red rushing blood coursing through her hand. A hand of exquisite beauty, graced with rather lavish rings of gold, silver and diamonds. I had never been touched this. way before and it made me queasy with excitement and apprehension. This lady was making advances toward me and there was no doubt about her intentions. What would I do now! What would I do!?!

I lifted my left hand to reach for my drink because it was, as if my right arm was paralyzed by her warm soothing touch, and besides, I didn't want to draw away, I was just scared a little.

"Why don't you come on upstairs with me for a little while'?" she said in her most sexy voice. We'll just rest a little and maybe have another drink. What do you say'?"

"I say okay, I guess, but what about Ben'?"

"Oh I've got a friend who can take care of Ben all right," and with a pert and cute turn she called over to a girl at the next table. "Carol, would you be a darling dear and come here please'? I've got a friend Iwant you to meet." And with that, Carol, excused herself and strolled ever so graciously over to our table and stood next to Gwen with her hand on the back of her chair.

"What can I do you for darling'?" She said as she surveyed the situation.

"My friend's brother here, Ben, needs a companion for the evening and I thought you might oblige. What do you say Sweetheart?"

"Oh yes, I think I would be up to taking care of some little old soldier boy off from the war, don't you'?" she said sheepishly and with a little rye sort of humor.

"Then we're off to never-never land you all. How about we see ya'll after a while." And with that, Gwen rose and took me by the hand and led me away and up the stairs and all I could do was just look back at Ben and Carol with a look like, well if you don't rescue me it's going to be too late 'cause I just don't have the strength or will to resist.

For some reason, money was never discussed that evening as we entered Room 18, the number an omen of legality, I thought. The things that happened behind that closed door I could never discuss with anyone, but I can tell you this much, that in the nocturnal mystery of that momentous event, I underwent my own sort of "baptismal of fire" in the comforting arms of the most beautiful woman I had ever known. It was a time I shall never forget.

That night I slept like a baby until dawn when I jumped up out of bed, put on my clothes and washed my face and combed my hair. I went over to kiss Gwen, who was still sleeping and lying there like a goddess. She was dreamingly drawing her right hand through her tossled blond hair as her eyes half opened and saw me kneeling down to her side as she smiled.

I said "Gwen, I don't have much money. I know I'm supposed to pay you or something. Here's a dollar. It's all I have."

She didn't say a thing at first, she only shook her head "no" and smiled at me and then she said, "Let's just say it was for the war effort, ok?" and with that she touched her lips with her two fingers and then reached out and touched mine. "Take care of yourself, soldier," she said.

"I will and I'll always remember you Gwendolyn, . . . always and forever." Those were the last words we ever said to each other and I never saw Gwendolyn again after that, but I would always cherish her sweet memory over all the years to come.

As I made my way out the door of the saloon and onto the porch sidewalk I found Ben sitting on the steps leaning against the wooden post. He looked pretty contented, if you ask me.

I said, "Well, how did it go last night brother? Was she all you could ask for? Did you really do it?"

"Well she was all I could ever ask for alright and it was sure some fancy time, but you know, I think I must have passed out somewhere between getting upstairs and finally getting into bed.

I mean, Carol was a handful if you know what I mean, but somewheres along the way things got mighty fuzzy. Guess I did it though! 'cause I sure don't feel lacking for anything this morning!"

I just listened and raised my eyebrows a little as I looked at Ben and shook my head in agreement. "Yeah, I know just what you mean big brother. Same thing must have happened to me!" And with that said and out of the way we never discussed the incident again.

It was Sunday now and the last day of our furlough. Ben and I both thought that since we had been so sinful on Saturday and Saturday night that at least we owed equal time to the betterment of ourselves. After all, we certainly weren't heathens not by a long shot. At least we didn't think so, but we figured we could do some good by going to a real bona fide church for Sunday morning preaching. It had been so long since we had heard a real live preacher that we probably wouldn't recognize one if he hit us right in the head with the Good Book itself Nevertheless, after asking a few directions and looking for the corresponding steeple we located the First Methodist Church of Augusta, Georgia. There were lots of people going in and it appeared that we were just right on time for the Sunday morning worship service. We entered through the great wooden double doors and found a partially filled pew toward the back. There were other soldiers there too, scattered throughout the congregation, so we didn't feel quite so conspicuous in our grey uniforms. Folks spoke to us from all around until the singing started. We must have sang a dozen hymns before they called for the offering to be collected. The offering plate was approaching me only two or three pews up and I realized that all I had was that one dollar in my pocket that I tried to give to Gwen. Maybe I should just give it, but a whole dollar was an awful lot to give to a church you didn't really know and besides, it was my last dollar. If I didn't I would I be shot dead in the next battle I was in and my soul go to Hell because I kept it for myself? Hell no, I wasn't going to keep that dollar for me, no way, I wouldn't have had it anyway 'iffin it" hadn't been for Gwen. No this dollar had to go in that plate and that was the end of self discussion about that and with a quickened reflex I reached in my pocket grabbed the dollar just in time and practically threw it into the collection plate as it went by me and on to Ben. Ben just passed it on to the next fellow without barely a thought or mind. Well, I thought, he would just have to live with his own self about that. Maybe he had to spend his last dollar or maybe he didn't. We didn't ever talk about it.

Finally, the preacher commenced to preaching, and he preached and he preached, and he preached. "The Bible," he said, "was the living Word of God and everything that proceedeth out of the mouth of man was to be inspired by God and judged by Him in every way. No man could take it upon himself to be his own counsel when it came to the security and spirituality of the soul. God would be the judgment and God would provide the punishment or the reward. Amen and Amen." That, I believe, was the essence of the service that morning, and by a quarter till one o'clock everyone was a mite ready to go eat I think. 'cause after the altar call, which lasted another twenty minutes, The benediction was said, the doors flung open and everybody flooded out the doors like the torrent of a great river current that had been released from a dam. Thank goodness, sometimes, that Sunday was only once a week.

Boy, we were starved and ready to get some grub of some kind. It didn't much matter what, but first we had to see if Ben had any money because I had put that last dollar in the collection plate. Fortunately, somehow, Ben still had about two dollars and some odd coins, so it looked like dinner would be on him. We found a little place and chowed down for our last civilian, meal for a while. We had to report back to camp by sundown, so that afternoon we just drifted along Main Street and back toward camp. We discussed whether or not we should call on the Langford family again and we both decided, not this time. They 'surely wouldn't be back anyway just since Friday morning. We'd try them another time. After all, we both had a lot on our minds by now.

CHAPTER 15

The Army Forever

Believe it or not the camp actually looked good as we arrived "home" and found our old familiar friends, and surroundings. It seemed like we had a great adventure in town and we really did, but now it was time to get back to the war.

We got a pretty good nights sleep that evening/ even after we had told our friends about all our adventures. Well, not necessarily about everything. Discretion was the better part of valor I had always heard and it seemed to apply in this case. The night was cool, peaceful and restful.

Morning came bright and early and old Sergeant Masterson was already kicking his heels up in the morning air.

"Get up you sorry rascals, you pitiful excuses for soldiers," he yelled at the top of his voice as he made his rounds from tent to tent. Reveille was blowing on the bugle but there was usually no big hurry.

"We're moving out!" came his next words. "We're hitting the road by noon! Breaking camp! Orders!" He barked. This time the sound of the bugle took on a new meaning.

Just where we were going was never said. South? North? East? or West? Who knows. Just movin' again. Part of the strategy of running an army, I presumed, was to never let the enemy know where you were or how many of you were there. It was all a big guessing game. Worked too, I guess, 'cause old McClellan of the Army of the Potomac had grossly over estimated our forces a number of times we had heard. It was a good thing for us too 'cause in reality his numbers were vastly superior to ours. It would have been a hard lickin' to have beat them on several occasions. This time we didn't have to worry too much about that because all the armies seemed like they was so scattered here and there all over the place. But then too, you never knew when you'd meet up with some blue-bellied yankees and have to yank their teeth out.

For days and days we marched and it began to be obvious that we were headed either for Atlanta or maybe up by Marietta way. We were going west and that would be a logical place to pick up additional supplies and munitions. Although we were pretty well supplied from Augusta, and we were ready for action if it was encountered.

The pace of the march picked up and by early September we had already been by Atlanta and Marietta and on our way to meet the Federal Army somewheres up toward Chattanooga but we didn't know exactly when or where. It appeared that Chattanooga had fallen prey to the Federal Army and that it was making a move south and possibly would try to drive its way all the way to Atlanta before we could stop them. But by about the middle of September we caught up with their little prank at a place which would, henceforth, always be called Chickamauga, after the Indian name of the little creek which, ironically, meant "River of Death". At first, the fighting was just a skirmish kinda like at Gettysburg, but within hours, it too had escalated into a full fledge battle.

The 9th Georgia Light Artillery was now joined up with General Braxton Braggs Army and it was the Confederate strategy to catch the advancing Federals off guard and lure them into the folds of the Confederate Army. It all seemed pretty good, except that the engagement was made a little premature, according to later estimates. This battle turned out to be one of the most fierce and bloodiest battles of the war as men on both sides were spread out over almost a forty mile front and by the time the forces consolidated all hell had broken lose.

Our artillery was directed along the center line of the Federals up on a slightly higher ridge to the west of our position. We let them have everything we had in the initial bombardment 'til our boys began to make their advancement. Finally, the advance was so concentrated that the Federal line collapsed under the heavy assault and actually withdrew from their position leaving somewhat of a gaping hole in the now divided Federal Line. It would seem that the yank was now in a really difficult position and he was. There must have been something like 50,000 men on each side of this engagement and all havoc was breaking lose as the Federals began a withdrawal toward the little town called Lafayette. Except that the left flank of the Federal line stood firm on a little hill called Snodgrass where General Thomas defended his position 'til the withdrawal could be completed and 'til nightfall, when he too withdrew. For his famous stand that he made under heavy and enduring fire he would become known later as "The Rock of Chickamauga" among Yankee circles.

One brave Confederate hero would emerge from the assaults on Thomas' position, a Major Herbert W. Kelley, who 'cause of his determination and persistence, would later become a Brigadier General. This gentleman I had great reverence for and respect as, I personally, had the opportunity to meet him on one occasion after the battle during an encampment. He was from Pickens County, Alabama, and had been raised as an orphan by his aunt and uncle. He was a self made man and a good soldier who I admired greatly. His personage and countenance would become somewhat of a mentor for me as the war moved on from battle front to battle front.

By now we had intelligence reports which had trickled down through the ranks that the Federal Army was, once again, occupying Chattanooga. Confederate forces soon occupied the crest of Lookout Mountain and Missionary Ridge overlooking Chattanooga down in the basin, sort of. By the latter part of November, 1863, the Federals had mounted major assaults against Lookout Mountain and Missionary Ridge. The Federals defeated our forces at Lookout Mountain, some had called it "The Battle Above the Clouds," 'cause it was so high up and sometimes the Confederates couldn't even see the Yankee blue lines as they charged up that mountain. They had done almost the same thing over on Missionary Ridge on the east side of Chattanooga and had finally driven our boys back into a retreat and off the ridge by the following day. Now the Yankees seemed to be entrenched in, at Chattanooga and it appeared they would spend the coldest part of the winter there since they now controlled the supply routes on the Tennessee River and had good rail service from up north. It would seem that the yankees were getting ready for something even bigger, and it would' have to be pretty soon.

For the winter we would camp in the vicinity of Dalton, Georgia, creating a temporary stalemate for the two armies. Before long, a new objective would be determined and we'd be at it again.

During all this time we had heard good reports on damage inflicted by General Wheeler's Cavalry, which our pa was riding with. They had wreaked havoc all around the enemy in Chattanooga and at one point had destroyed three hundred supply wagons with teams of six mules each making over 1800 mules destroyed also. Break the back of the supply line and starve them out was the philosophy of those actions and it almost worked. Probably caused the Federal army to make its move earlier than actually anticipated.

CHAPTER 16

The War Comes To North Georgia

Nowhere was the south more vulnerable now than in the tender heart of North Georgia. In the peaceful green hills of our homeland the ravages of war would take a mighty toll. In quiet places with obscure names that most of the world had never heard of before. Places like Resaca, New Hope, Picket's Mill, Allatoona Pass, Pine Mountain, Lost Mountain and Kennesaw Mountain, Kolb's Farm, Ruff's Mill, Nickajack Creek, Peachtree Creek, Decatur, Ezra's Church, and Jonesboro. All preludes to the ultimate fall and surrender of Atlanta, Georgia, itself. Few corners of the world, either before or since, have seen and been the object of more destruction and devastation due to the ravages of war than my own homeland.

Charred by the fires of death and christened by the rains of spring the death angel came with all his fury to lay waste and havoc. Some called him Sherman, others just called him "Fate" and still others refused. to believe that the sanctity of this great land had actually been invaded by the blue devils from hell,

The struggle went on for a long time. The major force of the invasion was met with resistance around Dalton, Georgia, and later Resaca, where a major engagement took place. Unable to defeat the Confederate Army head on, the Federals, ultimately, attempted a flanking movement around to the side of the Confederate lines. It worked, and the blue line advanced south. The whole tenor of this campaign would be mostly a long series of flanking movements to the south.

Movements and engagements around some of the most formidable earth-works and entrenchments ever built by the

Confederate Army or any other. This was guerilla warfare fought in a wilderness of heavy forests, few roads and not too much open country as most of North Georgia was farmed in smaller parcels due to the terrain. It was, most of the time, very hilly if not downright mountainous.

The Confederate victory at Resaca would soon be of little consequence as the grey line retreated to New Hope Church, near Dallas, and made another frightful stand against the advancing blue bellies. For two days we fought tooth and toenail with the yanks over hilly terrain and fallen and broken trees, laid into the advancing enemy to impede their progress. Our batteries did considerable damage against the enemy but the general topography of terrain would not allow for the proper and more expedient use of artillery. It was more as if we were firing giant pistols at close range and we were constantly in danger of being run over by the enemy ourselves.

Soon the Federals were trying another flanking movement around the Confederate right at a little place called Picket's Mill. It was there that our batteries were directed across a rather steep ravine in order to enfilade the enemy with cross fire in front of the Confederate line if such an advance should take place and it did. It was an awful site as the yankees moved forward and across that wooded ravine. They were met, not only with a very stiff resistance from the Confederate grey line, but they were also blasted with canister fire from our batteries on the side in one great blur of confusion and destruction. Must have been over 1,800 men of the enemy decimated by our fire. The flanking movement against our line had failed this time and on the next move we would have to be side-stepped again.

Later, I would discover that my mother's great uncle John Henry Gordon was shot in the left leg at New Hope Church and would be discharged among the wounded to return home as best he could. At the time we didn't even know we were in the same battle. But that was sort of the way this war was, with almost a hundred thousand men fighting in total on the two sides. We had probably forty to fifty thousand soldiers and it was like a large city of military personnel being constantly moved and shuffled around wherever the need called for.

Cassville had fallen hard to the Federals also before New Hope Church, and the little town had taken a terrible beating from Federal artillery. Mr. Cass, the namesake of Cassville, being a northern sympathizer, had taken off for the northern territory and later the town and county of Cass would be renamed something more appropriate for a southern community. The ladies academy there, being on the hills along the Federal battery placements was saved from burning, but the rest of the town almost in its entirety was destroyed by fire.

The route of advancement would force the Federal army to move along the rail supply lines, as this was part of the idea in being able to support the trailing Federal army from the rear for as long as possible; although, this would become increasingly more difficult as the army moved further and further into enemy territory, our territory.

By the time the Federal army had advanced across Cass County and down to Dallas in Paulding County, we were getting closer and closer to home. As our farm was just below Powder Springs, which was just south of Dallas. How far would we go? And where would we end up? Would we be fighting right on our own farm homestead in a few days? It looked like that was exactly what was going to happen.

As things would have it, we entrenched again around the hills just south and southeast of Dallas, Georgia. We, as mostly always, had very good defensive positions but rather poor positions for an offense against the enemy.

At Dallas, however, there was a rather rare Confederate offensive tactic in the charge of what most called, the Orphan Brigade, a regiment from Tennessee and Kentucky made up mostly of orphans from those states. They made a vicious and valiant charge against the Federal line, just south of Dallas across some considerably bad terrain, including a big hollow with a ravine in the center. Their advancement was noble and to be admired by all but it added little to the solvency of the Confederate position and the losses were very great.

Twin Peaks of Kennesaw Mt.
Looking from the Family Farm.

By the early part of June, 1863, the two opposing armies were already in the vicinity of Lost Mountain and Pine Mountain. On a clear day you could see Lost Mountain from the top of the hill near our farm. The armies were spread out across a wide front in this tag match of touch and go fighting, shoot and flank and re-entrench tactics. It was working sort of for the Confederate army, this defensive strategy, but we were losing ground almost every day. There was almost constant skirmishing all around the area as the two lines moved back and forth sort of along, maybe a twenty mile front, give or take.

Over on Pine Mountain, I heard we lost one of our best and most ablest generals, General Leonidas Polk, who took a cannonball right through the belly. It happened while he was standing on the hill surveying the countryside. Old Uncle Billy, as the yanks sometimes called Sherman, observed Polk and some other high officers on that hill, and just for the heck of it, directed that a few artillery rounds be dropped their way. And boy did they hit the mark.

Signals were sent to General Joseph E. Johnston, now atop Kennesaw Mountain, and it was said that he was mightily distressed at hearing the news about General Polk.

Now with Johnston on Kennesaw, the Confederate line swept around like a great snake from Marietta, up and across Big Kennesaw, down and back up Little Kennesaw, up over Pigeon Hill and southward over Cheatham Hill and on over to Kolb's Farm. This was now a consolidated twelve mile front. Less than twenty miles from home. As a matter of fact, we could always see Kennesaw Mountain on a clear day from our upper fields on the farm. Sometimes, I would remember just stopping to look at her and admire her, like she was some mysterious and majestic lady way off in the distance. I had never suspected in a million years that one day I would be a part of a major battle over the possession of her twin peaks.

It had fallen our lot to position the cannons up on top of the mountain and across the ridges to the south as far as possible. Because the enemy was to our front, the cannons had to be pulled by ropes and man power up the steep southern slope of the mountain to get them into the proper positions. This was a difficult and arduous task which took us over rocky terrain and sometimes a slope exceeding forty-five degrees or more.

I sure never thought that we'd be dragging cannons up this rocky mountain by hand! This was the pits, if you asked me, but the only question was would we get them in position in enough time to do some good. Well, yes we did and you talk about a defensive position, we had one. And also we were in a good position to be very aggressive with the artillery pieces. What with four pieces on top of; Big Kennesaw and four more pieces atop Little Kennesaw we were in an excellent position to overlook the Federal activities and we began a careful and methodical bombardment on key elements of the enemy below. We had other artillery spaced out along the twelve mile front all the way to Cheatham Hill. And with our men in gray, snugly entrenched just below our artillery we were truly ready for the enemy. It would only be a matter of time before the Federal line would make its move against us.

We figured that Sherman would definitely make a move on our position as we commanded the entire area and held the key to Marietta, a major stronghold before Atlanta. Although the conditions were most unfavorable for the Yankees, they had historically been rather successful in similar situations, like at Lookout Mountain and Missionary Ridge, especially. They were not going to be overintimidated by this little mountain, as precipitous as it was over the surrounding terrain. One disgusting soldier, undeserving to wear the gray uniform, said, that them Yankees weren't going to pay no more attention to this little hill than if it were Governor Joe Brown himself! I thought that was mighty irreverent talking about the governor of the great state of Georgia, even if he had been something of a hardhead about certain things, like being selfish with the state defense arsenal.

Ben and I were doing our duty with the artillery, but sometimes we hankered to be down there with the infantry where it seemed the real fighting was going on. But every day old Sergeant Masterson would remind us of how important our jobs were and how the infantry couldn't make it without the artillery and how proud we should be of the fine job we were doing. And I guess we were, it was just all so formalized and organized it seemed. We ran those batteries like machines. Machines of death and destruction. And we did a good job.

When we first arrived at the top of the mountain it was during the night and all was darkness as we began to make the final preparations on the gun pits, which had already been dug and built pretty much during the hours before. By daylight we were able to look out across the great expanse of the countryside below and we could see how very beautiful the north Georgia land really was. For all the times we had looked at and admired the Mountain, we had never ascended her slopes and seen what real visionary treasures lay exposed at the summit. To see them for the very first time under these circumstances and conditions was most unusual we thought.

Within a couple of days the blue forces were swelling below us and it was rather obvious by now that the Yankees just couldn't stand to not take a stab at us. It would be a fool hardy attempt by Sherman to make a frontal assault on such a defensive position, but then it never had stopped them before, so what would be different about this time, they, no doubt, thought. They would make the assault and they would make it soon. It was hot by now around the last of June, 1864. The war had been stubbornly going on for more than three years.

On June 22, General Hood, under the command of General Joseph E. Johnston, was directed to pull his forces from the Marietta side, around the southern side of Kennesaw and to the south at Zion Church, where he was to prepare to engage the Yankee line at or near Kolb's Farm. This precipitous assault on the Federal right lines would culminate in two unsuccessful attacks with heavy losses to the Confederates. As we found out later the unsuspecting Confederates were going up against a well entrenched Yankee line, and over fifty-two artillery batteries were bearing down in both a direct fire and an extended line of enfilade fire designed to catch the Confederates in a heavy cross fire, which they did.

Although the assault at Kolb's Farm was costly to our side, it did tend to stem the flanking of the left Confederate line at that time and evidently caused the Federals to have more confidence in making a frontal assault themselves.

By June 27 all hell broke loose and the Federals began to mount an assault like you wouldn't believe. From where we stood, we could see blue lines moving in great force across the fields below moving toward the base of the mountain.

We were directed to place as much fire as possible on these moving lines which were constantly being followed by more and more forces. We were getting off approximately three rounds per minute, which was right at our maximum rate of fire. The barrel was getting extremely hot as it always did at this pace of firing and you had to be careful that you didn't accidentally place your bare hand on the almost gleaming-hot iron. The constant barrage of roaring explosions, as the cannons fired, took a heavy toll on your ears which sometimes would bleed from the repeated concussions. And what was worse, was that there was hardly any break in this infernal pounding of artillery and musketry fire.

We could see the blue regiments moving forward on our lines across the fields and up the base of the slope. Somewhere along the base of the mountain we began to lose sight of the blue bellies due to the remaining trees, but at that point our rifle pits were well covered all the way over the slope and we began to cut them down like rats in the woodpile. But there was so many that they just kept a comin,' wave, after wave, after wave it seemed until the whole of the area was saturated with musket fire coming and going. It was like Gettysburg, but in reverse, as this time we were the well protected and the well entrenched defensive line on a steep mountain.

The Federals no doubt, thought that, like Missionary Ridge, they would just overrun us with numbers, but it wasn't working here at Kennesaw Mountain. The Federals would advance so far and then they would fall back for a while. In a little bit, here they would come again with new vitality and renewed determination.

The bullets were passing in the trees and overhead like a

tremendous swarm of hornets all around. And the sting from one of those hornets could, and often was, very deadly.

Zing, zing, zing, whiz, pow, pow, pow, went the barrage and counter-barrage of heavy rifle fire.

Our artillery fire was still being directed above our own line and onto the enemy in the open field above, designed to inflict as much additional damage as possible. And I believe we were doing a pretty fine job. Sherman had made a bad judgment call this time and the Federal losses multiplied.

We were also picking up some Federal artillery fire with exploding shells toward the top of the mountain for a while when they were trying to cut down our positions and knock out some of our batteries, but because of the steep elevation, the Federal artillery was mostly ineffective.

Over on down the line, we heard that a major assault, or rather the bulk of the assault, was taking place against the lower slopes at Little Kennesaw, Pigeon Hill, which was much lower and full of great boulders, and even further over at a place which was to become known as Cheatham Hill. The assaults in these places and especially at Cheatham Hill were massive and unbelievable as we were told. The attack on Big Kennesaw, where we were with our battery, was really a feigned attack while the real business was being conducted on the lesser slopes. But in all this time the gray line never broke.

After a long and drawn out effort of almost two weeks of this kind of stalemate, Sherman decided to turn his attentions elsewhere. He began to withdraw into a great flanking movement once again and he moved his army south and southwest toward Powder Springs and toward the Chattahoochee River. He would just do the old dancing sidestep one more time.

From then on, we too, had to take a new posture and retreat in order to protect our territory. Although we had been successful, even victorious, at Kennesaw Mountain, still it mattered little in the overall consideration of stopping the advance of the enemy.

Of course Atlanta, the heart of the great south lay behind us and across the Chattahoochee River. Our movements and activities now would carry the two armies, parts or whole, to new places with new names like Smyrna, Ruffs Mill, Nickajack Creek, and the Chattahoochee line just on the northern side of the great Chattahoochee River, last stopping point before approaching Atlanta.

There would definitely be fighting and various levels of skirmishing in all these places as the massive Federal army moved around like a great sloth destroying and absorbing all in its path of resistance.

Federal cavalry raids were sent out all through the area to gather food stuffs, foraging they called it. There probably wasn't a house, farm, village or whiskey still untouched within fifty miles either side of the great blue monster.

I know our own farm must have been raided for anything useful they could find, although it wouldn't be much at our place, and they probably burned the house and barns just to spite. We hadn't heard any word from the family, what with all the goings on and being constantly under attack or pursuit or entrenching a new position or on the move.

We hardly had time to spit in between minor engagements. We had heard that Salt Springs had been invaded and Sweetwater Town and even New Manchester, where Ma and Anna were working in the factory mill, and that the Federals had captured and burned the mill and most of the town. We could only hope and pray that Ma and Anna and the others had somehow safely escaped to Campbellton or maybe to Columbus or West Point. We prayed for their safety everyday.

It had been sometime now since we had heard any word from Pa, who was still riding with General Wheeler's Cavalry, which was doing much damage to the perimeters of the Federal army and causing great havoc on their supply lines. But we didn't know exactly where they were or how Pa was doing. We could only hope and pray.

Also Will, and Samuel and Levi were out there somewhere. Who knows where? How they were doing was only a guess by now. This war had really torn our family apart and it might be years, it seemed, before we might all be together again, if ever.

But we didn't have much time to be depressed or think about it all, as we too, every day, were fighting for our lives and our army and our beloved southland. Where would it all end? What would be the final outcome of this great travesty that had divided this nation and had pitted brother against brother and father against son within many families. Thank goodness, our family, was all southern, and we were sticking together in this fight. If we died on the battlefield or elsewhere it would not be by the hand of our own family.

The days passed and as they did the armies jockeyed for positions of defense and offense. Within a few weeks the Confederate Army had moved across the Chattahoochee River and set up new defensive positions along the eastern outskirts of Atlanta along a little creek called Peachtree.

By now it seems that President Jefferson Davis had become disenchanted with the maneuvering tactics of General Joseph E. Johnston and had replaced him in command with fighting General John Bell Hood, whom he knew would engage the enemy as he had at Kolb's Farm and other admirable attacks. He was definitely a fighting soldier, and now more than ever before, President Davis was wanting a fighting offensive, to ward off the ever advancing Federal Army. After all, he reasoned, that if Atlanta fell, the south might well be doomed and he was probably right in that thought. Much debate ensued over General Johnston's replacement, but perhaps it was time to make a change. Something had to be done. But it seemed that circumstances were not to favor our great southern army.

After the Federals also advanced across the Chattahoochee River and set up for a line of attack, Hood ordered a Confederate assault from Peachtree Creek and all hell broke loose again. The fighting was fierce and conducted through and under the cover of much undergrowth of vines and trees and scrub, often so thick that the enemy was laying into each other without notice or forewarning. There was a lot of hand-to-hand fighting and musketry fire at extremely close range. It was like fighting in a briar patch. After several unsuccessful assaults, at considerable loss, Hood ordered a general withdrawal back to the more established Confederate lines.

By now the Federal army was swinging around the Atlanta fortifications to the northeast side toward the settlement of Decatur where another major offensive by the Federal army was taking place. The fighting was awesome and centered around partly a stately new home that was ironically under construction by the Hurt family. It would be devastated in the conflagration that ensued as the two armies moved back and forth attempting, among other things, to gain or keep control of the Western and Atlantic Railroad which ran through Decatur from Augusta on its way to Atlanta. This too would cut off a major artery to the central nerve center in Atlanta. And having accomplished this, the Federal army moved around further to the east where the battle continued in what was to become known as the Battle of Atlanta, where the living, dead and wounded were all immortalized in the fighting around and for Leggett's Hill, one of the last bastions of defensive positions held by the Confederates. Thousands died, thousands more were wounded and thousands of others would live to fight again another day at Ezra's Church on the west side of Atlanta, and at the Battle of Jonesboro on the south side. There, at Jonesboro, General Hood attacks the Federal army with a result of heavy losses and the Federals gained control of the Macon Railroad and the Rough and Ready West Point Railroad. The seal of fate is finally placed on the city of Atlanta, Georgia.

On the night of September 1, 1864, the Confederate Army evacuates the city of Atlanta, blowing up valuable and badly needed ammunition stores and supplies, so that they will not fall into the hands of the enemy on the morning of September 2, 1864, Federal troops moved into the city and began formal occupation. On September 5, President Lincoln declares a national day of celebration to celebrate the fall of Atlanta and several other Union Victories, such as Admiral Farragut's victory at Mobile Bay.

Though the south has been severely wounded, the war will rage on for some time

CHAPTER 17

The Bleeding South

Atlanta has fallen and all hope of saving the great city from the devastation of the yankees has fallen with her. One of the last great bastions of Confederate resistance is now in the hands of the enemy. But the Confederate armies are still intact, if somewhat diminished in numbers.

General Lee and the army of Northern Virginia are still fighting up north somewhere and other armies and regiments are scattered all over the country. We happen to be here in an evacuation from Jonesboro, Georgia.

It is our understanding that we will make our way out of the supposed path of the Federal Army and somewheres toward the north. We have done all we can do right now under these circumstances. We have fought hard and long with all that we had. We did the very best that each man could do against overwhelming odds and a well supplied enemy.

As we make our way northerly and around the western side of Atlanta, up toward West Georgia, we see many signs of death and devastation as a result of the Federal raiding parties over the countryside. Hardly has a significant farm been untouched in some way. Many houses and barns have been burned in retribution for socalled uncivil acts by the civilian population against the occupation and presence of the enemy.

As we arrive at Campbellton, Georgia, along the south banks of the Chattahoochee River we witness the ravages of war which have been indirectly visited upon that little town, the county seat of our own Campbell County. Only the churches and the Masonic

Lodge remained standing along with a few homes. All the other public building and places of mercantile have been burned and destroyed. A policy of scorched earth, Sherman called it. Take the war to the civilian population and make them pay for it. After all, Sherman said, "War is Hell."

Ben and I decided since we were so close to home and in particular to New Manchester, that perhaps we could get a short furlough to visit Ma and Anna, and check on them and be sure they were all right. Fortunately, we secured a three day pass and it would be our responsibility to catch up with the regiment wherever it was as it headed on northward.

So, after taking a ferry across the river we headed up a ways toward New Manchester. Now, just up the river was the confluence of the Sweetwater Creek with the Chattahoochee River. From there all we had to do was go up stream several miles to get to New Manchester.

But first, we would arrive at the site of the old Alexander's mill, which had, been burned to the ground along with the miller's house and the few outbuildings. All destroyed. Ben and I were anxious for the safety of Ma and Anna and we wondered what had happened at New Manchester.

There was some evidence here and there of some rather significant fighting that had gone on evidently in defense of the mills. Ben and I didn't even know that there had been any fighting over around these parts but later we were to find out that there had been a fair amount. Nothing major like we had seen but still just the same a good bit of skirmishing and such.

Arriving at New Manchester we found a ghostly and ghastly sight. The formerly magnificent, five story, mill factory of New Manchester was nothing but a somber blackened ruin of standing bricks with no insides, no floors, no wood and no roof. Every inch of flammable wood had been burned and charred out. The remains of the walls stood as a silent testimony to what must have taken place. There was no one around to tell the story. Everybody was gone. Even the dogs.

The Company Store and all the houses had been burned to

the ground also. There was not one single standing structure left. Foundations lay like dead comrades in arms, slain by the oppressors. Silent and smokeless chimneys stood as deaf mutes shocked by the horror of what must have happened. The only sound, on this otherwise bright sunny morning was the roar of the river as it rushed ever onward over the shoals and the gentle breeze blowing carelessly through the great trees, many now also killed and dead from the apparent great heat of the fires.

We finally found the remains of the house that Ma and Anna were living in with Martha Jenkins. There was nothing. We could only conjecture what had happened and we figured that all the occupants of the town must have fled south to Columbus, West Point or perhaps Macon. Surely Ma and Anna and the others were safe.

After surveying the general grounds and rubble, we decided to go on up the creek to Mr. and Mrs. Ferguson's home and Mill and see if perhaps we could find Mary and Angus.

About a mile up the creek we found a similar sight, only in a smaller scene. The mill and their home had been burned and destroyed also. No sign of life existed except for the birds singing in the trees and the rush of the river. It was all so eerie. What had happened to everyone? It was truly a mystery.

Ben and I decided to camp there for the night and the next day we would go into Salt Springs and find out just what had taken place. Surely someone would be in Salt Springs.

That night as the Whippoorwills began their almost mournful laments, Ben and I sat close to the campfire and talked about the war and all the circumstances and situations we had been in and the close calls we had had ourselves. I didn't really want to, but I couldn't help crying over all the tumultuous circumstances. It was just too much. Finally, I too fell asleep in the deep of the night—there on the bank of Sweetwater Creek, and my thoughts faded into the obscurity of the darkness.

The sun rose lazily the next morning as it nosed its way through the tree limbs and scrub brush on the opposite ridge across the creek. There was no hurry, no early morning bugle call, no shouting to get moving, nothing, except the sweet songbirds of morning heralding the creation of another day. Ben and I both awakened as though we had been in some drunken stupor the whole of the night before. It would take a few minutes before the solitude of tranquility could be shaken off and we could get our wits about us. Today we would travel on up to Salt Springs to investigate just what all had really happened around there.

About three miles up the road we came into Salt Springs, the sleepy little town we had known in our childhood before the war. The little town, what it was, was surprisingly intact and appeared to be relatively unscathed from the ravages of War. There were a few scattered homes here and there and the livery was open, as well as, the blacksmith shop, but that was about it. The old brick factory had obviously been burned and was only charred remains. The Bowden house and Post Office were still standing as they were, one and the same.

Everything looked fairly normal to us, as far as we could see. We had seen a few folks here and there, but nearly all the fields we had seen everywhere were laying fallow with almost no one to work them. Normally we would have seen local farmers and even city folks working their fields, for now we were in late harvest time, but there was little or nothing to harvest after the yankees had been through. It was most eerie to see in our imagination the ghosts of so many dead soldiers working their fields, as over ninety percent of all soldiers in the Confederate Army were farmers just like us.

The big trees surrounding the Bowden House Post Office were a welcome sight and the shady grove they created was a comforting sanctuary for the lingering citizenry as everybody picked up their mail and whatever news they could from long seen love ones. Actually, we too, were more anxious to see if any mail had arrived for us or any of the family, than we were to talk immediately to any of the folks standing around the grounds, of which there were only a few scattered about.

We walked in the door of the two story piedmont plantation style house, and taking off our caps and carrying them in our hands, we rather slowly and reservedly made our way over to the grilled box that served as the official post office. No one was there so we rang the little bell that was provided.

Ding! No one came.

Ding! Ding! Ding!

"Ooookayyyy Okayyy" Hold your horses, be there in a minute" came a gruffled old voice.

About that time, from the back of the wall came old man Bowden himself, looking just like he did a hundred years ago, only older and a little more frayed around the edges.

He leaned back his head to lift the lower part of his bifocals so as he could see just who we were and what we wanted.

He squinted his eyes a little and made a little expression of surprise on his face which was followed by the most delighted smile and countenance.

"Why you're R. B. Jett' s boys, aren't you sons?"

"Yes sir, we are."

"Let's see, you're the youngest boys aren't you? Ah, Ben and Steven, I think."

"Yes sir, Judge." You know, he really was a judge too, and we wanted to be mighty respectful.

"Do you have any letters for our family Judge?" we asked with great anxiety.

"Well boys, I don't know, a lot has been going on around here lately. There might be, yes, it seems that there have been several letters to come in over the last few months and no one has picked them up since, lets see, since I guess the Yankees came through back in June and July. Matter of fact boys, this isn't really a safe place for two Confederate soldiers to be, even if you are on a furlough or something. I'd be a might careful around these parts 'cause yankee patrols have been allover the area. Not as bad now as it was, but still the same, you need to be careful."

"Yeaaaah", here they are. I'd just set them aside for you, figured somebody'd be here sooner or later to claim them for the family. You can just take them all, there's four letters here. Good luck and God's speed boys, blessings on you and your family, let me know how everybody's doing."

We thanked the Judge and taking the letters, we turned and walked slowly out the door and back into the outside light where we could see good to read the outside of the envelopes.

Four letters. One, two, three, four we counted together. Addressed as follows: Mrs. R. B. Jett on one, Mrs. R. B. Jett and Family, on another, Mr. William Jett on another, and Mr. Steven Jett and Mr. Ben Jett on the last one. Who could that one be from!

We too, like the others around, found us a good shade tree and we settled down to read the news, thinking that it was our family duty to open and read all the letters, even the ones addressed to Ma, since we didn't know where anyone was or just when we might see any of the family again, if ever.

We figured that we'd save the more personal letter to us for last and that we'd start out reading the letter to Ma. Ben would read the first one, and then I'd read the next. The letter read as follows:

May 10, 1864

Dearest Wife,

Please know that I am well and in good health. I hope you and the children are also. I worry a lot about the boys off in the war and I worry a lot about little Anna. Although I expect she is quite the young lady by now.

We have moved since I wrote you the last time. We are now camped on the south bank of Holston River at a Methodist camp ground I wonder why it is I haven't heard from you lately. Let me know if them seed I sowed before I left home is likely to grow.

When I get in reach of home I will come home some morning before day and wake you up with sweet kisses.

Give my Love to all,
Your Loving Husband
R. B. Jett

"Okay Ben," I'll read the next one. I'm gonna read this one from Will.

August 30, 1864,
Fort Gilmer

Dearest Mother and Family,

We have been on the move here lately from the Beautiful Valley of Virginia to our present position southeast of Richmond where our Company B is in charge of the artillery. We are in sight of the yankees and though several shells have been thrown into the fort, there has been no attack since I have arrived.

There is fighting nearly every day. Sometime in sight of our lines of breast works and that of the enemy is close to each other and extend a distance of 30 miles along the countryside. Heavy cannonading is going on all the time.

I am so sorry that you all have had some of the problems you have had. It is grief to me to know that the enemy destroyed all you had to live on. God knows, I would be so glad to see this cruel war come to a close so I could return home to my family. Don't be uneasy about me, as I haven't taken up with bad habits so commonly practiced in the army.

I will write again as soon as I can.

My Love to All,
Will

"So William has ended up in the artillery too!" How about that Ben! I said.

"Yeah, I hope he likes it better than we do," Ben said.

"Let's see this one now!"

And Ben began to read aloud.

August 15, 1864

My Dearest William,

"Oh boy this is going to be good," said Ben.

Yesterday was a day I'll never forget in a million years. The Yankees have been bombing us here in the city for several weeks now. The first person killed by an exploding shell was a little twelve year old girl down on Mitchell Street. I don't know who she was but they said she was one of Mr. Hardy's nieces and that she was working in the general store for him part time during the summer to earn money to go to art school. What a pity!

But, yesterday William, I went down to Mama Leana's house to get some butter and when I got there the whole house had been destroyed from bomb shells. I looked around as best I could until under some big boards I found a foot sticking out and I just knew it was Mama Leana's, and it was. She wasn't dead yet, but she was all bloody and had a great big gash in the top of her head and her arm and both legs were broken. I tried not to panic but ran to get help.

We got her out and over to a makeshift hospital at the Christian Church so the doctors could see her, as they were so busy already with the wounded and all.

The doctor dressed her wounds and put splints on her arm and her two legs and said it would have to be up to us to take care of her from there on and to watch for fever set tin' in cause it probably would.

After three days if she has survived she'll need to see the doctor again, but only God can know if she will live through all this, especially at her age of 74.

William, I miss you so much! My heart nearly breaks with hurt and the not-knowing where you are or that you are well. I wish we had gone ahead and gotten married before the war cause we may never have a chance to consummate our love for each other.

I am so sick and tired of Atlanta and all this so-called siege. Some days we get almost 5,000 shells a day and we have to live in holes in the ground like they did in Vicksburg. A lot of folks evacuated the city but most felt that our army will be able to defeat the enemy and save our splendid city. We can only pray to God for its salvation.

I have to go—please write me and tell me you are still alive and how much you love me, as I must have some comforting words from you.

All My Love Now and Always,
Sharon

"Well well—ummmmm" I said"

"Yeah, that's old Sharon Hamilton isn't it ?" said Ben.

"I remember her. Don't you? She came out to Salt Springs one time with her uncle to look at some mules and that's when her and Will met down by the creek when their wagon broke down. Remember?"

"Yeah, I remember all right! She's all Will could talk about for two weeks and then he started to court her over in Atlanta didn't he?"

"Yeah, sounds pretty nice though. We'd better save this for Will. I just hope he doesn't get pissed off for us reading his mail."

"Nawww," said Ben. "He'll be alright. After all, we are his brothers you know. We got to look out for each other," he said with a grin and then a big smile.

"Okay, let's see, we got one more to us," said Ben. "Let's flip to see who reads it!"

"No, go ahead, you can read it," I said. "I'd rather listen anyway!"

Grave Robbing at the Bowden House

July 4, 1864

My Dear Steven and Ben,

Hope this letter finds you two in good spirits and in good health. I was so sorry to have missed you boys last fall down here in Augusta. When I got home Lucy told me that you had come by and she even gave me the whistle you made for me. Works pretty good. Thank you very much.

I was going to write sooner, but I really didn't want to get caught up by two soldier boys like you even if you were real cute. I figured like all the other young men you'd just go and get yourselves killed or something. So I didn't really want to experience the pain. Selfish of me I know but that is the truth. But tonight was the 4th of July and I couldn't help but remember the exciting time we had at cousin Stephanie's up in Atlanta and how we watched the colorful explosions and held hands.

Ben I adore you, but Steven I love you with all my heart. I miss you so much and would like to see you again as soon as this stupid war is all over. Stephanie plans to have another big party soon, as it will be her birthday November 4 and we plan to go up to Atlanta to celebrate her 18th birthday. Please write to me and try to come to Stephanie's birthday party if you can. I will not rest one minute until I see you again and know that you are all well. Until then I will carry your whistle with me every day and when I blow it I'll be calling you home.

Love to All,
Debbie Langford
Augusta, Georgia

"Boy! Hey, how do you rate so high up there!?!" Ben exclaimed. "I don't know," I said, "Just lucky I guess. Very lucky indeed!"

"I can't get over that!" said Ben. "She was suppose to be in love with me. Really though, I like Stephanie. She's more my type."

"Boy, my butt's about wore out," I said, as I got to my feet. The late morning sun was moving across the sky and the early morning shade had shifted to the east.

We'd have to be going soon because we had to be back to our unit by sundown the next day.

We were getting our things together when, out of the blue and with no warning whatsoever a yankee calvary patrol came riding into the yard of the Bowden house. Must have been about fifty riders it seemed, just all of a sudden. Ben and I decided to sit back down under the darkness of the shade tree and try to look as unobtrusive and as inconspicuous as possible. We'd probably stand out like a sore thumb. It was too late to run' or try to hide.

The Captain, I supposed, rode up to the steps of the house, got off his horse and handing his reins off to an adjutant, walked inside. They were carrying the colors of the 5th Kentucky Calvary.

During the meantime the men sort of spread out and some rode over into the small family cemetery just across the way. A few men got down and began removing the top slab of a sarcophagus so as to expose the inside. They were being rather rambunctious and carrying on considerably. Suddenly, one of the soldiers takes a rifle butt and begins hitting it against something inside. We hear the crashing of glass breaking. Then he reaches down and pulls out this gold watch and chain and holds it up like it was some kind of treasure he had just captured.

"Ain't no dead rebel gonna need this no more!" he shouts.

About that same time some old timer walks over and sits down by me and Ben and watching the action, begins to tell us that old man Bowden's son-in-law, Captain Summerlin, had been shot and killed at the Battle of Kennesaw Mountain and that he had a young baby son. His mother wanted him to be able to see his father when he got older so they had buried him above ground in the sarcophagus in a casket with a glass window in the top. Evidently the yanks had heard about it from somewhere and had figured on robbing the grave.

Ben and I did have our muskets down at our sides and we did

have a couple of side arms, but we knew we'd be no match for a whole cavalry detachment. All we could do was watch the indignity perpetuated on the fallen comrade.

It had been a common practice for the enemy of both sides to rob the dead of any treasures found and this was not too different, although it really stuck in our craw to see this happen not more than two hundred feet away.

While all the commotion was going on, we figured we'd use the opportunity to try to slip away and we sort of excused ourselves and told the old man to watch our cover as we tried to escape.

Just as we were moving back and down the way behind us down toward the privy hedge, some yankee blue belly saw us and headed our way. We made it to the privy hedge and quickly hid in the bushes.

About the same time the captain had come back out of the house, put on his gloves and remounted. Upon remounting he quickly turned his horse around and bounded off in the opposite direction away from the house. The other soldiers followed except for the one who was trying to find us. We laid low and did our best to not make any noise that would give us away. By that time Ben and I both had our hand guns out and ready for whatever might be required. The privy hedge was so thick that the horse couldn't maneuver through it so the yank dismounted and began to frail through the hedge trying to flush us out. By now, maybe five or ten minutes had passed, and we figured that the rest of the raiders were on down the road by now. This raucous looking yankee was cursing up a storm at us and demanding that we come out and surrender ourselves.

We stood fast and just as the yankee finally opened up the last bushes with his saber, hacking away as he came in. BANG! KAPOW! Went the unmistakable screaming roar of a single round from Ben's Army Colt 44 calibre revolver.

The bullet entered the middle forehead of the yankee and blood rushed out in a great burbling spurt, as his eyes opened wide and white in unbelief and he slowly slumped to the ground.

Boy we've done it now I thought. "They're going to be back on us like ducks on a June bug!" I said "Let's get out of here!"

By that time the old man, who had been talking to us, caught up and told us to go on and get out of here and that he would take care of the dead yank. He'd get a shovel and bury him right there under the outhouse, a very appropriate spot and nobody would ever be the wiser.

So we thanked the old man and decided the best and only thing we could do was to get out of there as fast as we could. We grabbed up the yank's horse and Ben jumped on first and then me behind and we rode off double carrying our muskets and gear as best we could, headed for home which was in the opposite direction the raiders had gone anyway.

Three miles west we came to our gate at our fence line. The old house was about another thousand feet down the white sandy road. The fields were all grown up from neglect and the vines and grass were out of control everywhere, but it was home. The main house and smoke house, well house and corn crib were all ok, but the large old barn had been burned to the ground. The house door was open and the house had obviously been ransacked and looted. All the livestock was gone, the chickens and even the dogs were gone. Probably been shot for target practice. We'd heard that the yankees did that just for fun and sport.

We were both tired and depressed to see our farm in this sort of condition but it really was good to be home for the first time now in almost two years.

We decided not to hang around too long, as the raiders might be on our trail and we needed to get on back to our unit, so we soon rode out, leaving the farm and our memories behind us.

CHAPTER 18

The Road to Nashville

The pain of defeat lingered in our minds and bodies for weeks after the fall of Atlanta. Ben and I were no different than other soldiers and we too felt our pain at seeing our homeland taken and destroyed so mercilessly. As we made our way back to our Army of Tennessee we saw destruction everywhere. Homes and barns burned and fields destroyed. But things were not over yet.

The fourth day morning about 4;30 A. M., we finally found our unit as it had been moving around quite a bit. It had last made camp just west of Salt Springs a ways, at a place generally called Skint Chestnut. The army was fairly spread out but we were able to finally locate our unit, the 9th Georgia Light Artillery. First thing we did was report in to Sergeant Masterson, who reprimanded us at first for being late, then congratulated us on finding them at all that soon.

"Get some shut eye for a few hours if you can, we'll be on the move again soon I expect," he said in a fatherly sort of way.

By the next evening, we had made our way to a place called Dark Corners, where we set in for camp for a day or two. We didn't know for how long, but we had heard that we would be making a move on Allatoona Pass, where a Union supply depot was now stationed along the northern railroad and Federal supply line. General Hood, who still commanded the Confederate Army of about 30,000 men or so, hoped to draw Sherman out from Atlanta and to have the opportunity to reengage him in the rolling hills of north Georgia, once again, affording him the opportunity of defeating the Federal Army. This could be possible as it seemed that Sherman's objective, all along, was to engage and destroy us, the enemy, which he had only partially done up to this point and time. Soon the enemy was to be engaged at Allatoona Pass and Sherman had already sent part of his army, northerly from Atlanta, under command of a General Schofield, in pursuit of General Hood.

The garrison at Allatoona ·Pass was under a greatly fortified defensive position although they could not match the numbers of the impending Confederates. An opportunity was extended for them to surrender and avoid a bloodbath, but the commander declined, as he had already been signaled from Sherman, atop Kennesaw Mountain, to "Hold the Fort!"

And hold the fort he did, after a very heavy and costly assault by our boys, who were ultimately unable to break their lines of defense, due to the restrictive topography of the pass itself, and finally the assault failed.

We must have put a hundred rounds of fire from our cannon alone into the mouth of that pass and it did no good.

During the melee, Sergeant Masterson caught a random shot mini-ball in his right shoulder and he began to bleed profusely.

I grabbed him up, yelling, "The Sarge has taken a ball!" Get me a compress or something! I grabbed up a piece of jacket that had been thrown down and immediately began to press it onto the wound to suppress the bleeding. Evidently an artery had been severed from the way it was bleeding. He'd probably lose his arm at least if he didn't down right bleed to death. We got him over to the side and up against a tree and made him as comfortable as we could until the fighting was over.

After the battle we were gathering up the wounded and Ben went over with a friend of his George Scott, to check on Sergeant Masterson.

He was so still.

"Hey!" George yelled, the Sarge is dead I think. He won't move!"

Apparently, he had gone into shock after loosing so much blood and unable to suppress his own wound had just slowly bled to death. We all felt so bad, like it had been our fault or maybe if we had been able to do more we could have saved him. We had by now known of a lot of men to die in battle or from wounds but the Sarge had truly been—like a father to us all. George, in particular, just broke down and wept.

"He was a good man," said Ben.

"Yes, he was a very good. man indeed," I agreed, as we proceeded to carry him to the back lines. He was from Oconee county, Alabama, and we knew he would want his family to know the circumstances of his death. It would be up to our commander to make the full report and to notify the family.

Things were not the same now that Sergeant Masterson had been killed. George Scott was promoted to Sergeant to take his place but he really didn't want to be no Sergeant. By now we were just all doing our jobs like some kind of animals. All we did was fight and march, eating when we could and when we had the food. If we didn't have it we just skipped eating, but we never skipped fighting or marching.

By now we were well on our way to Nashville, Tennessee, to attack the Federal Army there and Sherman's men had already turned tail and went the other way back to Atlanta. He obviously had other plans of some kind.

By mid November, 1864, we knew that Sherman had forced the civilian evacuation of Atlanta and had set it afire destroying nearly the who1e of the city or what was left of it. He then set out for the Georgia coast across the great state of Georgia with nothing between him and the Atlantic Ocean but the "Fat of the land" to live on and feed an army of 60,000 men. They would cut a swath about 60 miles wide and lay total waste to everything in their path. With no opposition, Sherman would arrive at the Atlantic Ocean and capture Savannah, Georgia right at Christmas time, when he would present the city as a Christmas present, on December 24, 1864, to President Lincoln.

We, under the command of General Hood, would press on toward Nashville by way of Spring Hill and Franklin. The Army of Tennessee still had a lot of fight, even now, and we were ready once again to engage the enemy. Hood was just looking for the right opportunity and he finally got it at Spring Hill. But, before the lines could be put in place for the attack, the Federal Army, under General Schoflelld, made a night-time escape, less than 600 yards away from our advance pickets, away from Spring Hill and into the town of Franklin. By the next day, November 15, 1864, all the Federal supply wagons had crossed over the Harpeth River and the troops were well entrenched on the south and west sides of town with very good defenses. General Hood was so mad that he ordered 18,000 men to attack as soon as possible. By three o'clock in the afternoon the Battle of Franklin had begun. It would rage on for six hours until around nine that night.

The fighting was fierce and covered a fairly long line. Our job, as usual, was to pound the tar out of the enemy positions as best we could. We took some fire ourselves but were a moderate distance from the heavy fighting.

Five great Southern Generals would die in this one battle alone. They were 0. F. Strahl, States Rights Gist, John Adams, H. B. Granbury and Patrick Cleburne. The latter two generals had led, among other things a brilliant defense in the Kennesaw line at Cheatham Hill against five brigades of assaulting Federals. But Franklin would be no match for fortitude or fame and the battle would claim its own day of infamy. At the conclusion of this battle, the five generals would all share the same make shift morgue, being the front porch of the Carnton home, just on the outskirts of town, along with 1,500 fellow comrades to be buried in the family graveyard. Over 8,500 casualties would be suffered from both sides. About three Confederates for every one Federals. It was a devastating blow to the Confederacy, and what is worse, is that during the night, Schofield pulled right out of Franklin, abandoning his positions and moved right into Nashville, where he joined up his 25,000 men with General Thomas' 30,000 men already entrenched and vastly fortified.

Supposedly, Grant had ordered Thomas to attack us but for some reason he was taking his own sweet time. And sure enough, it was working for, instead of against him. Now with Schofields troops he had amassed a sizeable fighting force against our own dwindling strength of about 23,000.

Hood was caught in a classical sort of stalemate. He was overwhelmingly outnumbered, so a frontal assault on Nashville would be really strategically unwise, and yet he had nowhere else to go. It was doubtful that he could muster an orderly retreat of his army due to the circumstances. So we waited for almost two weeks, when finally, on December 15, 1864, Thomas ordered his own attack against our positions just south of Nashville.

Starting out in a dense fog around 6:00 A. M. our lines were first attacked by negro troops of James B. Steedman against Cheathams division on the right. Yes, the one and the same, Cheatham of Cheatham's Hill fame at Kennesaw. This would be a secondary action while the main force of the Federal attack would fall against our weaker left line, and then a hard attack at the center. Somehow, and I don't know how we did it, but our artillery unit of 148 men held off a 4,000 man Union infantry division for two hours, before the left line began to fall apart. Cheatham was brought into the center to reinforce the position but when Schofield's Federal Reserve was brought in the odds were too great and Hood ordered a retreat.

By nightfall, Thomas was sure he had defeated us, but he hadn't. By the next day we had moved two miles to the south and were ready again.

The Federals once again moved on us in great force although we had formed a shorter and much stronger perimeter. The progress of the battle this day was slow and delayed. One Federal assault on the right had been thrown back by our boys who were doing just fine, until almost at the same time, two impatient yankee Generals decided to storm the steep hills on, our left line with two brigades about 4:00 P. M. We can't believe it, but spectators are over on the far hill yelling and cheering on the Federal troops as they make their way up the steep slopes. within a very short time they are at the top and waving the Stars and Stripes in mortal defiance of our now estranged line. About the same time the right line gives and flags, not ours, are waving over there.

It appears that the Union Flag is all over and that our lines have fallen indeed. Before loosing our entire army, Hood orders a retreat and a heavy rain begins to fall. Our spirits are dampened both inside and out during that gloomy and deadly afternoon.

This would be the last real battle of the war that me and Ben would fight in. For us the war was essentially over. This final battle ultimately left the whole of the Army of Tennessee routed and in final disarray as we retreated to the south. It would be the end officially of our army as we knew it. Hood would soon resign his command and every soldier was on his own, more or less.

It was almost Christmas time and nearly everyone headed for home or other parts unknown. Some units stayed together as best they could. Many were captured by the enemy.

In our own case we had to abandon our cannons and left the batteries to the discretion of the Federal Army. We skedaddled as fast as we could to the south. Stragglers would be picked up by the Yankees over the next several days, for those who hung around. We sure didn't want to see the inside of no yankee northern prison!

We crossed hills and dales, creeks and dense underbrush as we escaped toward the south. About twenty miles away we met up with other soldiers who had reconvened into smaller separate units, totally unorganized and with little purpose or direction at this point. There was three of us, me, Ben and George Scott who had stayed together, and we decided to camp for a few days with this group we met up with on the bank of a fair size creek. It was a beautiful site to camp and would make a good place to rest up for a few days.

Most of the fellas were from the infantry from a number of different units. It wasn't long before we were making new friends and all discussing the previous battle and other battles and about the whole gall darn war and what we were going to do now.

We all set around large group camp fires with lots of talk way into the night. Several men had volunteered to serve as pickets around our perimeter, for whatever good it would do. I never heard so much mouth at one gathering of men ever in my life. We heard about everything, from what I would consider stupidity, to down right treason! Some wanted to surrender, some wanted to fight. Some just didn't give a damn anymore what happened!

Mostly, Ben, George and me just listened and every once in a while we might interject a word or two, but nothing profound. By the following day everyone pretty much decided that we'd all head toward home, and then if we wanted to rejoin with some other outfit we would. Most of the men had fought some long and hard campaigns. They were tired and worn out. There was no supplies, no food, and no munitions. Many were barefooted. We were no army now! We were just a bunch of evacuees. So either one by one, or in small groups, they began to leave the camp over the next few days. After the third day, we decided we too, would head for home.

All I can say, it was a long walk home! We kept mostly to the back roads and camped in the woods at night. We had to be careful not to expose ourselves too much, for yankee cavalry patrols were all through the area and we had to avoid certain parts entirely.

The news of the rest of the war that we picked up here and there wasn't too good either. General Lee was having a terrible time and everybody said it was only a matter of days before it was all over. The South would not win this war. The odds now were too great. There was not enough left of us or our supplies to last much longer. Georgia, itself, had been invaded and cut completely in half by, Sherman's Army who was now fighting in the Carolinas. Richmond, Virginia, the capitol of the Confederacy was barely holding on and Lincoln had been re-elected. It seemed we were doomed!

As we moved south, Ben and George and me got to talking and we decided, for us, that it wasn't over until it was over. We would move toward Virginia and try to meet up with some of the other boys up there. After all, somewhere out there was Will, Samuel, and Levi and Pa. As long as they were fighting we would fight with them if we could find them.

Over the next several weeks we moved toward Virginia, ragged and torn and tired but still willing. Our progress was slow and the only food we had was what we could find or kill along the way. It began to seem like a futile effort. We were making such slow progress that we figured maybe we should just try to catch up with some of our boys in the Carolinas, if possible. By the middle of February we met up with the army of Joseph E. Johnston in South Carolina. We joined up with a regiment of irregulars made up of mostly Georgia boys from past scattered regiments like ours. We were issued weapons from fallen comrades, and ammunition and food, that was about it. Our commander was a white haired older man named Col. Reginald Davis, whom we understood had seen a lot of action throughout the war. He was a good man with an even temperament and good disposition. We would do good under his leadership. We were ready to do whatever had to be done.

Sherman was moving out of the now captured Charleston, South Carolina, where all rail lines had been cut and the city had succumbed to the Federal occupation. Now even Fort Sumter flew the Federal Flag once again.

As Sherman cut his way across South Carolina, he pushed Johnston and our army into North Carolina, where in the later part of March, 1865, we would once again meet the enemy face to face at Bentonville. The only hope was for Johnson to be able to move far enough north and Lee far enough south to join forces. Then we might have a chance. A real chance! A last hope sort of chance! But that, it seemed, was not to happen.

At Bentonville our army of gray was faced with overwhelming odds and the so-called battle ended up being a series of defensive maneuvers as we were forced to fall back into retreat even further. Much like the tactics of the old days in North Georgia, only a year earlier.

By mid April, word had come that General Lee had surrendered his Army of Northern Virginia at Appomattox Court House, Virginia, on April 12, 1865. Our fate was sealed and a few days later General Johnston surrendered our army to General Sherman and the war was over. Really over!

CHAPTER 19

The Aftermath

These had been difficult years for everyone. There was hardly a family in the South or North who had not been touched in some way by this terrible war. Aside from the physical brutality of the war itself, there was the mental anguish of dealing with the physical loss of health and family and homes and nearly all personal possessions of any kind.

We still didn't know what had happened to Ma and Anna, Pa, Will, Samuel or Levi. Somehow, you just go on without thinking too much, in the hope that they are all right. During the war itself, we didn't have much time to think anyway. We stayed pretty busy looking after our own hides, but now the war was over. A general armistice had been proclaimed and it was time for all soldiers of the south and all but the regular army of the north to go home.

On the 25th day of April, 1865, we mustered out of the Confederate Army. We were permitted to take with us all our personal gear; weapons if any; any food available; those with horses were permitted to keep their horse, so as to return to farming as soon as possible. The day we left camp was a dark, gloomy day, with it threatening to rain almost all day. It was a time of both sadness and joy inside. Sad, of course, because in finality, our cause was lost, but on the other hand, joy, because now maybe things could get back to normal. Or could they? Could things ever be normal again after something like this? I doubt it seriously. This was only wishful thinking.

The road back home was long and difficult. There was no

longer the army to look for to direct our purpose or needs, Many of the boys couldn't accept the fact that the war was over and that we had lost or been defeated or given up, whatever had happened. The truth was almost impossible to believe.

For the next several weeks, we, like thousands and thousands of others, made our slow and painful way across the forlorn southern landscape. Some would have homes and family to return to, others would have only parts of families and pieces of homes to return to, and still others would have nothing at all.

We by-passed Augusta, Georgia, on the way home, as it just wasn't in our hearts to go there this time. We made our way as quickly as we could back toward Atlanta, or what was left of Atlanta, our last big stop before home.

When we got to Atlanta, we found the city, much as we had heard, in a state of depression and misery. Most of the city was destroyed and burned with charred remains everywhere. Hulls of once formidable buildings standing empty and hollow, with only silent brick and stone walls remaining as testimony to the devastation of Sherman's army. Many homes, in fact the fair majority of homes, had been burned to the ground. People were living in huts and shacks of makeshift debris and in small camps around and throughout the city. There was a sort of vitality and urgency to the activity which permeated the city, something like a three legged dog trying to keep up with the day to day demands of survival. By now, people had returned to the monumental tasks of cleaning up and rebuilding, but it would be a long and slow progress for quite a while.

While we were there, we decided to look up Herron's Restaurant, Stephanie's family business, down on Luckie Street, but it too was not to be found. As a matter of fact, the entire area had been totally destroyed. It was so unbelievable! How could almost an entire city just be wiped off the face of the earth? We tried to find their home up on Peachtree Street, but it too, became painfully obvious that their home no longer existed either. The splendor and beauty of all the fine homes was gone. Only charred remains and an occasional tall standing chimney were all there was to be found. We asked some questions regarding the Herron family but nobody knew where they were or anything about them. Most people, we were told, had just left the city for other safer places. After the war now was over, perhaps they would return, but maybe they wouldn't. What did they have to come back to anyway?

"I bet they all went down to Augusta," I said to Ben.

"Yeah, probably did," he agreed.

"But you know, I don't know if I'd ever come back to something like this!" Ben said.

"Well, we did, and this is what we found. I wonder what we'll find when we go home, ourselves, to Salt Springs and the farm?"

"Couldn't be any worse than this!" Ben Blurted.

So with additional fear and trepidation we advanced on Salt Springs and home.

Within a short distance of the sleepy little town we could begin to tell that everything looked just about normal as far as we could tell. It was all pretty much like the day we had last been there back in the Fall of last year. The day we killed the yankee grave robber. Well, it wasn't actually the grave robber himself, but it was one of his cohorts, whom, we knew must have been just as bad.

We had barely escaped with our lives that day and at best could have spent the rest of the war in a yankee prison somewhere. Ben and I made a vow not to talk about the incident to anyone at all, due to the fact that there still could be possible repercussions. Although we considered it an act of war and not murder. Some things were just best left alone and this was one of those things.

We checked for mail at the Bowden house, but Mrs. Bowden said that there hadn't been any mail come in for months now, as she guessed all the service had been suspended. She was mighty glad to see us though and was so thankful that we had survived the war and all. She also said that we'd be pleased to know that our Pa was home, and had come by there about a week earlier, and to please give the message to any of the family. She also told us, as she had told Pa, that Mrs. Jett and our sister Anna, had been taken by the army, along with most all the folks from New Manchester, to somewheres in Marietta or Roswell and that they hadn't been heard of since. Rumors are, that the army sent them all up north somewheres so as they couldn't work in no more mills down here in the south. She hoped that they were all ok, but she just didn't know anymore. Can you imagine, herding people up like they was cattle or something, and just shipping them off somewheres else to a strange place or something, like they weren't even human. I mean these people were civilians, they weren't soldiers. They weren't any threat to the Federal Army! All forced against their will. This just didn't happen. We'd never heard of anything like this happening anywhere else during the war. Why here? We would find them somehow and we would vindicate their wrong! You could count on that!

The final walk home was the most difficult three miles we had covered, I believe, in all our journeys up to this time.

Our minds were so full of anticipation and anxiety that it was all we could do to contain ourselves. Each mile seemed longer than the last, until finally we arrived at our front gate. From there we made our long walk down the white sandy road which led to the house.

No dogs were barking to welcome our arrival, only the silence of the soft breeze blowing gently through the large old oak trees surrounding the house with the occasional sound of a spring songbird filtering through.

As we approached the front porch we saw the old familiar door swing open and a man we had never seen before moved slowly forward walking on one leg and a crutch. It was a man ravaged by the terrible cruelty and weariness of almost four years of war. It was like we had never seen him before, but it was our Pa.

As we hurried up the steps, he as best he could, moved to us and we all three embraced with tearful eyes and heartfelt thanks at our reunion. We began to laugh, almost hysterically for just a moment, laughing I guess at the impossibility of it all and how amazing it was that we were back on the farm, where only a short time ago we were only young boys with a young Pa. Farmers of the land, gone off to war and to return again, all as changed men. Men who had seen the "Elephant" and lived to tell the tale and a thousand and one other stories to share with our grand-children in the years to come.

Yes, Pa had lost a leg, but he had come home to his family. At least to where his family used to be. Now it was an incomplete family like a torn and ragged precious cloth which used to protect us all with surety and safety. Now we were broken pieces and we must each determine our future.

As soon as we could catch our breath and talk again, Pa and Ben and me began to talk about Ma and Anna and what supposedly had happened down at New Manchester and about Will, and Samuel and Levi. What had happened and where they all were. We had heard so little in the time we had been gone. We each had bits and pieces of information and we began to share what we did know.

Pa had received several letters from Ma and Anna from up in Indiana where they were living in a little town called New Albany. They were okay and doing fine, but they sure did have a story to tell.

Pa said, "As soon as I got home, provided I did get home alive, I was to write to her and Anna and let them know, so that they could make preparations to come home. I have written them and expect to hear back from them soon. God, in His providence, has protected them otherwise from many of the terrible things of this war. We can thank God for that much!"

Then with tears streaming down his iron hard face and with pain in his gruffled voice, Pa said "We lost Will, boys. Up at Petersburg just at the end of the war almost. He was working his cannon when a shell exploded overhead and he took home a mass of shrapnel. His commander said he was one of his best officers. He had made captain."

We were all silent at hearing the unsettling news about Will. There was nothing we could say, hardly. We knew first hand what it was all about and we always suspected that some of us would not return due to statistical impossibility, almost. We too shed our tears as we fought back the emotional trauma.

"Samuel and Levi, were captured by the yankees in some action up north I don't know exactly where or what the circumstances were," said Pa.

I haven't heard from them yet or any other news about them. I just hope they're coming home all in one piece. May God watch over them, is my only prayer.

"Let's go get some grub!" Pa said with as much enthusiasm as he could muster up. So together we fixed up the best meal we could with the meager provisions we had. It was a fine thing to be home on the farm once again. We would talk for long hours and share many stories over the next few days while we were getting reacquainted with our Pa. He was a little different now, as were both Ben and myself. We had all been through too much.

As we worked to put the farm back into some kind of order, the days drifted lazily by. It was time for spring planting, even though late, and we'd have to work hard to get some kind of crops planted in. We borrowed some seed from some of our neighbors and put in just enough for a good garden, as we didn't have any horse or mule to work the fields. We would be busy for a good while for there was a lot to do to put the farm back into shape. And every day we waited and watched down the long white sandy road for our brothers Samuel and Levi and for Ma and Anna. One day they would be back and we anxiously awaited their return.

Finally, one day we were chopping wood up by the long sandy road, when a noise was heard like someone shouting and a hollering. We looked up and saw the limping figure of a tall man coming down the way with as much speed as he could get himself going. It was Samuel! Good old Samuel! But where was Levi? We threw down our tools and ran to meet him like the long lost brother he was. When we got to him he was a sobbing and laughing at the same time, he was so happy to be home. He was a wretched mess with tattered clothes and barefooted and looked almost like a skeleton.

"Levi didn't make it ya'll" he said through his tears. "He caught pneumonia while in prison this past year and he just couldn't shake it! I done everything I could to save him Pa!" he pleaded.

"It's ok, Samuel," Pa said. "We know you done your best to take care of Levi. It weren't your fault!" And he put his arms around Samuel and hugged him tight and we helped him to walk on to the house. We filled Samuel in on all the news about the rest of the family. He couldn't believe it about Will and he was really upset too, about Ma and Anna and what had happened to them. It took days and days for the truth to settle in as we all tried to get on with the new work to be done, but our hearts weren't altogether in our work as we strived to rebuild our home and our attitudes.

It wasn't long before we got a letter from Ma and Anna informing us that they would be home around the first of June. The days were getting a lot warmer now and it was almost summer. The first of June had come and gone and we were still waiting. On occasion I would walk up to the high ground and look out across the fallow field and see the beautiful mountain. She was almost waving back on the distant horizon and she seemed to be talking to me and reminding me that she was still there and that the world was a good place to live. She said to me that life was good and precious and that there was a place and purpose for all of us. She said that life would be good again and that I too, would find my own destiny among the stars and hills of this great land.

With tears in my eyes and with sweat on my brow I looked the other way across the field and saw my beloved mother and sister coming down the dusty road. Both heavenly and earthly we were all home.

THE END